10,50

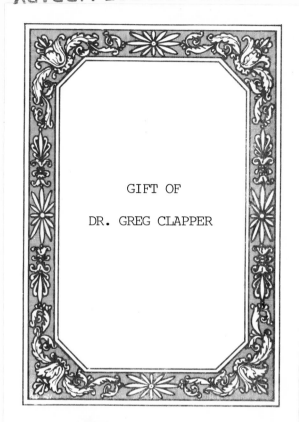

GIFT OF

DR. GREG CLAPPER

THE PRIMACY OF PRACTICE

THE PRIMACY OF PRACTICE

ESSAYS TOWARDS A PRAGMATICALLY
KANTIAN THEORY OF EMPIRICAL KNOWLEDGE

NICHOLAS RESCHER

89-624

OXFORD
BASIL BLACKWELL
1973

ISBN: 0 631 15020 X
Library of Congress Catalog Card No: 73–79629

Printed in Great Britain by
Western Printing Services Ltd
Bristol

For Gerald J. Massey
in cordial friendship

CONTENTS

PREFACE

The essays gathered in this volume were presented as a series of lectures delivered in the School of Literae Humaniores of the University of Oxford during the Trinity Term of 1972. I am grateful to the Sub-Faculty of Philosophy for inviting me to give these lectures, whose presentation proved a very pleasant occasion for me. I should like also to express my sincere thanks to Corpus Christi College for affording me an academic foothold during my stay in Oxford.

In general terms, it might be said that these essays develop in a more ample and emphatic form the pragmatic perspective of the idealist position of my earlier books, albeit in such a way as to keep the Kantian aspect at center-stage. Four of the eight essays are altogether new (nos. II, V, VI, and VIII), the others derive from prior publications, though generally in a substantially revised form. (Details as to the relationship of this material to the previously published versions are given in footnotes in the text.)

I am grateful to Miss Kathy Walsh for preparing the typescripts both for initial lecture-presentation and in revised form for publication, and also for helping to see this material through the press. And I wish to thank Mr. Brian Baker for his help in correcting the proofs.

INTRODUCTION

Though these essays cover a varied terrain, they have a definite unifying theme and a common objective. They argue the subordination in the sphere of factual knowledge of theory to practice, and stress the extent to which the justificatory mechanisms of our knowledge regarding the empirical features of nature are controlled and undergirded by considerations of practical reason relating to human purpose and human action. The pivotal purpose of the book is to maintain the methodological centrality of practically conditioned assumptions, postulations, and imputations as governing principles for the rational validation of our acceptance of general truths of fact, and in particular to highlight the important function at the methodological level that *regulative* principles—such (for example) as those of the Consistency of Nature and the Uniformity of Nature—play in our empirical knowledge. It will be argued in particular that various methodological presuppositions and postulates (of which these two principles are somewhat extreme examples) lie at the basis of our empirical knowledge regarding general matters of fact. Above all, I shall contend that the methodological groundwork of empirical knowledge rests in crucial respects on a foundation of practical principles, and shall accordingly maintain the fundamentality of practical and utilitarian considerations in the rational architectonic of our scientific knowledge of contingent fact. (However, it will be maintained that this fundamentality of practical considerations on the *factual* side does not carry over to the *normative* sector, where the controlling factors must—at least in part—be sought elsewhere.)

The essays included in this volume are of markedly Kantian orientation. But they are not, with one exception, devoted to the philosophy of Kant as such, but rather to applying certain Kantian ideas and theses to the elucidation of current philosophical issues. Pervading the whole discussion is the Kantian conception that certain fundamental assumptions or *postulates* underlie our empirical knowledge of what goes on in the world.

Correspondingly, a central place is given to the distinction between the empirical information that we *bring away from* our experiential encounters with the world, and the fundamental postulations (presuppositions, assumptions) that we ourselves *bring to* these experiences, and which will accordingly condition (i.e., in part determine) the characteristics of these experiences, as well as the information we derive from them. This conception that our empirical knowledge—and in particular our empirical knowledge of general truths—rests on certain *justified postulates* (of regulative import) regarding the nature the world is a continuing and fundamental theme of these essays, which accordingly have markedly Kantian flavor, not in the sense that they contain much exegesis of Kantian texts, but rather in their application of Kantian ideas in dealing with some current philosophical issues.

The reader will soon sense, however, that his dosage of Kant is administered with a heavy admixture of Peirce in that the invocation of methodological presuppositions and postulates is conditioned by the controlling considerations of pragmatic orientation—considerations of operative usefulness and efficacy. The pragmatic doctrine at work throughout these pages undoubtedly finds its precursors in the practice-minded post-Kantian tradition of Hegel, Schopenhauer, Peirce and his followers, and indeed even in Kant himself. It does, however, take a line markedly different from that of the classical American pragmatists at any rate, since ours is a *methodological* pragmatism that applies pragmatic standards at the level of the rational instrumentalities of inquiry, and is not a *substantive* pragmatism orientated towards specific theses about what happens in the world. (This feature is a point of strength in rendering our position immune from various criticisms frequently directed at the traditional forms of pragmatism.)

Thus, the orientation of these essays can be viewed from a Kantian perspective as effecting a closer fusion between the first two Critiques, stressing (in the manner of the first Critique) the *a priori* underpinnings of our *a posteriori* knowledge, but legitimating this on grounds which (in the manner of the second Critique) are not necessitarian and transcendental, but rather *practical* in nature. Accordingly, the move to the sphere of the practice-orientated considerations of the second Critique is made

But how could one meaningfully implement the justificatory program inherent in this question? Seemingly in only one way: by looking on the one hand at C-validated propositions and then checking on the other hand if they are in fact truths. But if C really and truly is our working criterion for the determination of factual truth, then this exercise becomes wholly pointless. We cannot judge C by the seemingly natural standard of the question whether what it yields as true is indeed *actually* true, because we *ex hypothesi* use C itself as the determinant of just this.

At this point it becomes altogether crucial that C really and truly is the criterion we actually use for truth determinations. Clearly, if someone proposed an alternative procedure C', the preceding methodology would work splendidly well. For we would then simply check whether the C'-validated propositions are indeed truths—that is, whether they are also validated by C. But with respect to C itself this exercise is patently useless.

It is difficult to exaggerate the significance of this extremely simple line of reasoning. It proves, in as decisive a manner as philosophical argumentation admits of, that our operative standard of factual truth cannot be validated by somehow showing that it does indeed accomplish properly its intended work of truth-determination.

So much, then, is a firm basis. But the problem of interpretation remains. In particular, the ominous question arises: Is the proper conclusion to be drawn from this argument the sceptical result that any and all rational justification of our standard of factual truth is in principle impossible? It is obviously important in the larger scheme of things that it should be possible to develop a line of argument against this sceptical conclusion.

2. METHODOLOGICAL INSTRUMENTALISM: THE PRAGMATIC TURN

Since a method is never a method pure and simple, but always a method-for-the-realization-of-some-end, the pragmatically teleological question of its *effectiveness* in the realization of its purposes becomes altogether central. It is thus clear that, with respect to *methodology* at any rate, the pragmatists were surely right: there can be no better or more natural way of justifying

Chapter I

THE PRIMACY OF PRACTICAL REASON

I. THE BASIC ARGUMENT

Let C represent the criterion we actually propose to use in practice for the determination of factual or empirical truth—whatever this criterion may be, that is, whatever sort of process or procedure governs our determination of such truths. Accordingly, one is to be committed to classing a fact-purporting proposition p as a truth if and only if $C(p)$, that is, if and only if p meets the conditions specified in C.

It will make no difference to our argument what the nature of C is. Whether it is first-hand observation, the standard processes of scientific methodology, the deliverances of immediate intuition, the indications of tea leaves, or the declarations of sacred sages, all this is totally indifferent for all immediate purposes. The discussion proceeds at a level of generality where no *particular* C is in view.[1]

Nor need C be uniform and homogeneous: it can be as complex and composite as you please. If you choose to divide the realm of potential fact up into a variety of themes or topics or subject matters, and apply an altogether different standard in each region—say a discursive process at some places and a direct one at others—then so be it. The standard C then simply becomes a complex composite of multiple subcriteria. Well and good.

All that I ask is that we be serious about C; that C really and truly is the criterion we are actually to employ in the practice for determination of factual truth.

How are we to validate our employment of C? Can it be shown that we are rationally justified in using C at all? This had better be so, considering our very libertarian approach.

Now to all appearances the question of the appropriateness of C is simply this: Does C yield truths?

---

[1] Clearly, however, one needs to impose on any proposed criterion C various formal conditions of eligibility on the logical side, e.g., that C validates only propositions that are mutually compatible, that when C validates a conjunction it also validates both conjuncts, etc.

already when dealing with the epistemology of objectively factual knowledge, instead of being postponed until dealing with the normative issues of ethics and theology. The unifying aim of these discussions is thus to expound and defend a Kantian pragmatism with respect to the methodological mechanisms that provide the rational foundations of our knowledge of matters of contingent fact.

a *method* than by establishing that "it works" with respect to the specific tasks in view. The proper test for the correctness or appropriateness of a method is plainly and obviously posed by the paradigmatically pragmatic question: Does it work—that is, does it attain its intended purposes? Does it deliver the goods? Anything methodological—a tool, procedure, instrumentality, program or policy of action, etc.—is best validated in terms of its ability to achieve the purposes at issue, its success at accomplishing its appropriate task.

The problem of a truth-criterion can be helpfully illuminated by viewing the issue from the perspective we obtain once we take the pragmatic turn. After all, a truth-criterion is at bottom methodological: it is naturally to be viewed as an *instrumentality* —one for obtaining truths, and thereby for realizing the sundry purposes whose attainment is the very *raison d'être* of our search for truth. But just what are the purposes germane to a truth-determination method; what is it we propose to do with the propositions that it validates to us as truths?

A justificatory analysis along instrumentalistic lines is invariably ends-oriented and purpose-relative. To say of something that it works or succeeds is to say that it is effective in realizing the purposes at issue. An instrumental analysis can only get under way when ends are given. It can, of course, evaluate mediate or proximate ends in terms of more remote, ulterior ones, but as regards the ulterior ends themselves it must look elsewhere.

These more or less truistic considerations lead straightway to the problem of the controlling purposes of the epistemological considerations canvassed in the present discussion. We must consider and resolve the question of the sorts of purposes at issue with respect to the resource of human knowledge.

This deceptively simple seeming question poses profound and far-reaching issues. In particular, it forces us to give prominence to a recognition of the tritely familiar but still fundamental fact of the amphibious nature of man as a creature of mind and body; intellect and will; reason and action; theory and practice.

Our knowledge answers to two categories of purpose, the theoretical and the practical. The theoretical sector of purpose is *pure* and the practical sector is *applied* in orientation. The theoretical relates to the strictly intellectual interests of man, the acquisition of descriptive information and explanatory understanding (to *what* and *why*); the practical relates to the material interests of man that underlie the guidance of human action: avoidance of pain, suffering, frustration, etc. The functional role of our knowledge encompasses both the intellectual/theoretical aspect of the purists' knowledge for knowledge's sake and the activist/practical aspect of knowledge as a guide to life.

This fundamental duality points to a correspondingly dual aspect in our acceptance of truths:

(1) On the one hand there is the *cognitive or theoretical* dimension of our concern for the intellectual aspect of information or knowledge. From the purely intellectual aspect of man as knower, success is represented by our mastery of correct information about things and failure entails the natural sanction of error.

(2) On the other hand there are the *practical and affective* aspects of man as an *agent*—as an actor emplaced *in medias res* upon the stage of the blooming, buzzing confusion comprising the goings-on of this world of ours. The critical element here is our welfare not as abstract intellects concerned solely to acquire information and avoid error, but as embodied agents concerned for their welfare in situations where failure entails frustration, pain, or even catastrophe.

Our acceptance or nonacceptance of truths, of course, has profound involvements on both the cognitive and the affective sides of the theoretical/practical divide, since such acceptance furnishes a guide both to belief and to action. Hence a truth-criterion comes to be endowed with a duality of objectives: Truth on the one hand is a standard of belief in purely intellectual regards, and on the other a guide for our practical life.

Now in the light of these considerations, it would appear that one way of drawing the moral of the preceding argument is not as establishing scepticism, but rather as showing merely that we cannot apply the conception of success in the *theoretical* mode of cognitive correctness as the justificatory standard for our criterion of factual truth. Since truths serve us amphibiously on both the theoretico-cognitive and the practico-active side, and since considerations on the former, theoretical side are seen to be inadequate to meet the needs of the justificatory situation, we are thrown back upon the latter, practical domain. One is accordingly led to surmise that the natural and appropriate step is to use success in the *practical* mode as the justificatory standard proper to a criterion of factual truth.

But how is such an approach to be implemented?

3. PRAGMATIC VALIDATION OF THE CRITERION OF TRUTH

The structure of the instrumental justification of a method/procedure/instrumentality inevitably conforms to a certain generic pattern. We begin with two items, a specification of the method M in question, and of the set of aims and purposes μ for whose achievement the method M is intended. The instrumental justification of M then takes the generic form of the following characteristically means-end reasoning:

(I) *M works (as well as any envisaged alternative)* for realizing μ. Therefore M is to be adopted-as-the-correct- (i.e., best or most appropriate)-method relative to μ.

Note this is a piece of practical reasoning in a sense approximating (though not coincident with) Aristotle's: the conclusion has to do with adopting a course of action rather than establishing a fact. Contrast the cognate reasoning:

(II) *M works (better than any possible alternative)* for realizing μ. Therefore, M is the correct method relative to μ.

This is not practical reasoning but demonstrative, and its conclusion does not indicate an action but a fact. (The establishment of the fact that the conclusion asserts, of course, has certain practical "implications," but this is always and inevitably so.)

At this stage, the focus of concern naturally converges on the premiss of the argument. What can "*M* works" mean in such a situation? Clearly, its meaning must be construed somewhat as follows:

(W_M) If a course of action instantiates M by conforming to the methodological precepts at issue, then it will (certainly, probably, as probably as any other) lead to the realization of the aims μ.

Thus the "standard task" of an instrumental justification—a task whose discharge is required to provide the premiss for an application of an inference-pattern of type (I)—is to establish the *success* (in the just-specified sense) of the method *M* at issue.

Let us apply these general considerations regarding methods in the abstract to our special case of a criterion *C* of factual truth, now regarding *C* as a methodological instrumentality of truth-determination. Of course, we must begin by specifying the relevant purposes for such a criterion, viz.,

(1) the *cognitive* purpose of affording the knowledge of truths: the purely intellectual aspect of providing information.

(2) the *practical* purpose of providing a satisfactory guide to our agency—i.e., a guide to satisfactory courses of action.

As maintained in the preceding section, our initial argument may be construed to eliminate (1) as a usable standard of assessment. Accordingly, it seems that we are thrown back upon an exclusive reliance upon (2), a circumstance that indicates the classically pragmatist test of a truth criterion as the natural recourse at the methodological level. At this stage, then, we make a transition from a generically *instrumental* approach to a specifically *pragmatic* one.

If we adopt this stance, and restrict the purview of relevant purpose for a criterion of factual truth to the pragmatic domain of practical purpose, then (W_M) comes to take the specific form:

(W_C) If we use the criterion *C* as basis for accepting a claim as to be acted on as true, then it will provide a satisfactory guide to action.

But now clearly, *if* the criterion *C* is itself simply that of practical success of "working out in the guidance of action," *then* the crucial premiss (W_C) comes to be altogether trivialized.

The pragmatic criterion of truth itself has therefore at least this merit, that its very nature is such that it will discharge the "standard task" of an instrumental justification. But it does so only too well. It provides a *logically tight* guarantee of validation for the essential premiss that the method in question works in terms of the relevant range of intended purpose. In adopting the pragmatic criterion we close the otherwise inevitable logical gap between the methodological instrumentality on the one hand and the realization of its correlative purposes on the other. But this fact is, in the present context, not helpful but unfortunate. Clearly, such an essentially tautological premiss cannot possibly provide the basis for drawing any substantively interesting and nontrivial conclusion.

The lesson of this line of thought must be construed as follows: That while the pragmatic validation of a criterion C of truth—at the methodological level—may well be a worthwhile venture when C is some standard other than the pragmatic criterion of truth, the pragmatic approach of criterial justification cannot possibly be fruitful when we contemplate the specifically pragmatic truth standard (with C as the pragmatic criterion of truth itself). Use of the pragmatic approach at the methodological level *preempts* its use at the substantive level. And since there seem to be excellent and compelling reasons for its employment at the methodological level, we would be well advised on this ground alone (not to speak of others at all) to write off the pragmatic criterion as a substantive test of truth.

Accordingly, the appropriate policy is to give a pragmatic argument not at the particularist level of justifying a *specific* propositional thesis, but at the *generic* level of a process for justifying theses-in-general. Thus (W_M) would take the form:

(W_C') If we use the (nonpragmatic) criterion C as basis for classing theses (in general) as true, then this generic process—this *general* policy—will provide a satisfactory guide to action.

Our pragmatism thus proceeds at the wholesale level of a general procedure, not at the item-specific level of justifying particular propositions.

A comparison may prove useful. The pragmatic theory of truth comes close to being the epistemological counterpart to ethical utilitarianism. Now it is well-known that utilitarianism can take two forms:

(1) *Act utilitarianism*, which asserts that an act is to be done (i.e., qualifies as morally right) if its performance is maximally benefit-producing.

(2) *Rule utilitarianism*, which asserts that an act is morally right if it conforms to ethically warranted rules, and

that a rule is warranted if its general adoption as a principle of action is maximally benefit-producing.

Analogously, pragmatism can take two forms:

(1) *Propositional pragmatism*, which asserts that a proposition is to be accepted (i.e., qualifies as true) if its adoption is maximally success-promoting (=benefit-producing).

(2) *Criterial pragmatism*, which asserts that a proposition is to be accepted (i.e., qualifies as true) if it conforms to an epistemically warranted criterion, and that a criterion is warranted if its adoption as a principle of propositional acceptance is maximally success-promoting (=benefit-producing).

When one considers *acceptance-as-true* as an act and looks—as it is natural enough to do—upon *classing a proposition as true* as a type of action, then the result of applying the utilitarian approach (in one or another of its forms) just is pragmatism (in one or another of its forms). And even as one can in principle be an act of utilitarian and not a rule utilitarian (or vice versa), so one can be a propositional pragmatist and not a criterial pragmatist (or vice versa).

But there is one crucial disanalogy. Our argument has shown that if one is a criterial pragmatist then it is altogether *pointless* to opt for a propositional pragmatism as one's specific criterion of acceptance because the process of criterial justification could not in principle succeed in this instance. On the other hand, if one were a rule-utilitarian then it would be not *pointless* but (presumably) simply wrong to opt for an act-utilitarian rule of conduct because (presumably) this specific rule would be invalidated on rule-utilitarian grounds. Adoption of the utilitarian standard at the level of rules does not *preempt* but rather (presumably) *invalidates* its use at the substantive level of act-assessment.

The shift from a pragmatism of propositional theses to one of criterial methods is crucial from the standpoint of rational legitimation. For when a *thesis* is at issue, the onus of justification lies with him who maintains it, not with him who chooses to call it into question. And this remains so even if the thesis is of a pattern whose instances have proven true on past occasions. But when a *method* is at issue—one that is established as "in possession of the field" on the basis of success in past applications—then the onus of justification moves from its adherent to him who chooses to call it into question. In this regard, the burden of proof comes to be shifted from the adhering to the questioning party when (generally successful) *methods* rather than (generally validated) *theses* are at issue.

4.   THREE STRATEGIES OF INSTRUMENTAL JUSTIFICATION

But how exactly is the pragmatic strategy of justification to be used with respect to a criterion of factual truth? If we are to implement and apply the line of reasoning inherent in an argument of the form

The method M works (in terms of its effective realization of the purposes μ)

$\therefore$ The method M is to be adopted (relative to a commitment to μ)

then we are, of course, immediately faced with the problem of obtaining its premiss. But how is one to show that a method M works?

Three possible alternatives come to mind:

(1)   *Demonstrative justification*
      To establish that M works as a matter of *logico-conceptual necessity*. (For example: a certain procedure for determining the roots of a cubic equation.)
(2)   *This-or-nothing justification*
      To establish that M works *on grounds of principle* as well as any method possibly can. Accordingly we are to show that if any method works then this one does:
      $$(\exists M) \text{ works } (M) \to \text{ works (this)}$$
      (For example: Hans Reichenbach's celebrated pragmatic justification of induction.) Note equivalence of this tactic with another: with—if this does not work then nothing works
      $$\sim \text{works (this)} \to \sim (\exists M) \text{ works } (M)$$
      or consequently—this works or nothing does:
      $$\text{works (this) } v \sim (\exists M) \text{ works } (M)$$
      This is exactly identical with the well-known this-or-

nothing mode of justification used by certain of the
English idealists for the justification of induction.

Both of these lines of reasoning represent a *theoretical* mode of
justification, and call for arguments that proceed on matters of
general principle. But a variant empirical rather than theoretical
course is also open:

(3)   *Experiential justification*
To show that *M* works *as a matter of empirical experience
as well as any other tried alternative*, i.e., that it has
proven itself in practice.

Let us now attempt to bring these abstractly possible alternative strategies of instrumental justification to bear upon the
specific problem in hand, viz., that of justifying a criterion of
factual truth through its success in providing a basis for action.
Unfortunately, it transpires that all three modes of instrumental
justification encounter substantial difficulties here.

5.   THE PROSPECTS OF A PRAGMATIC JUSTIFICATION OF A NONPRAGMATIC CRITERION OF FACTUAL TRUTH

Our approach to the validation of a criterion of truth regards
this criterion from a methodological angle as affording a *method*
of truth-determination. The structure of the problem is thus as
follows: One begins with some proposed (nonpragmatic) criterion
C of factual truth. The task is then that of showing that adoption
of *C* is successful in practice. Note that success here is *not* truth-
production (our earlier argument ruled this out). Here "successful
practice" should, as we have seen, be construed to exclude the
purely *epistemic* practice of knowledge-acquisition and may be
confined to considerations of *actual* practice: action-guidance as
assessed in the affective order of leading to physically and psycho-
logically satisfying results (no pain, frustration of plans,
unpleasant shocks, etc.).
But just how is this methodological metacriterion to be implemented? How is one to go about establishing that the adoption of
C as basis for guidance of actions is successful; that if we use *C*
then good results will ensue? Four procedures seem open to us.
The first of these is:

(A) *The Route of Necessity*
Give a logico-conceptual demonstration of necessity that:
If we use C, then we must necessarily have beneficial results (because action on C is *inherently* benefit-productive).

This necessitarian approach could succeed only if C were itself the pragmatic criterion, but this is not feasible for previously indicated reasons. And if C is not the pragmatic criterion but something else, then this necessitarian line of argument is not very hopeful. After all, we know that even if, instead of dealing with C-validated propositions, we dealt with *true* propositions pure and simple (never mind for the moment where we got them from—maybe God himself) then even this cannot provide an unfailing guarantee of practical success.[2]

Accordingly we turn to another justificatory procedure:

(B) *The This-or-Nothing Route*
This approach calls for establishing that:
If anything can produce success, then this C will produce success.
We are to show as a matter of principle that if any criterion whatsoever can deliver the goods, then the the criterion C at issue will do so.

Here C is validated by what might be called *the-only-game-in-town principle*. This approach may hold promise in theory, but in practice it seems methodologically over-ambitious. Its prospects are certainly not hopeful. How could one hope to demonstrate on grounds of general principle that C alone can prove benefit-providing?

We may thus proceed to the third prospective justificatory procedure:

(C) *The Dominance Route*
On this approach we are to establish on grounds of general principle that whenever C' is any method alternative to C that has some promise of success, then C will do at least as well as C'. Thus C has the feature of intrinsic noninferiority.

[2] I have argued this point in the chapter "Pragmatic Justification: A Cautionary Tale" in *Essays in Philosophical Analysis* (Pittsburgh, 1969).

This dominance approach may be more promising than (B) because it is less demanding, but is still patently overambitious. For it requires us to demonstrate a claim—viz., the predominance of *C*—that we can scarcely hope to establish on theoretical grounds of general principle.

Accordingly, it is well-advised to explore the prospects of an empirical and *a posteriori* experiential justification. For this approach alone does not share with the preceding approaches the feature of representing an *a priori* demonstration that proceeds wholly on grounds of theoretical principle. And it is problematic, to say the very least, to take the view that an operative criterion of factual truth can be validated by strictly theoretical considerations. We thus arrive at:

(D) *The Route of Experience*
This approach calls for an empirical justification of *C* on the basis of observed results. In effect we are to show that *C* has been tried and found to work out to satisfaction.

This experientially pragmatic line of attack suffers from various seemingly decisive impediments. In particular, three of these seem especially serious for this prospect of validating a criterion of factual truth:

I. An appeal to experience seemingly presupposes an already-established criterion of factual truth to tell us what experience has been.

II. Even if the employment of a criterion has been followed by good results, what guarantee is there that this success was actually produced by the criterion? *Post hoc* is not *propter hoc*.

III. Experience is past-oriented, but the justification of a method must envisage its future applications as well. Even if the criterion has worked to good avail in the past, what warrant is there for maintaining that it will prove successful in general? (Hume's Problem.)

The remainder of the chapter will for the most part be devoted to considering ways and means by which these three seemingly decisive obstacles in the way of an empirically based pragmatic validation of a criterion of factual truth can be obviated. For I want to contend that, its seeming disadvantage notwithstanding, this experiential route of justification is promising and viable.

6. THE PROBLEM OF PRIOR TRUTHS: THE PLAUSIBILITY OF MEMORY AS A MINIMAL REQUISITE FOR AN APPEAL TO EXPERIENCE

To begin with, one must face up to the critical point that any use of the instrumental approach to methodological justification which invokes the record of actual experience will require some empirically factual inputs. We inevitably have to talk about our own actions and subsequent developments. The instrumental defense in terms of the actually experienced results of adopting a certain method is given by fleshing out the schematic structure of the following skeletal line of reasoning:

(1) One specifies the method M at issue and also the appropriate family μ of its intended objectives and purposes.

(2) One adopts the method M as basis of operation towards the realization of μ—that is, one *applies* M in practice.

(3) One notes that none of the promising methods M', M'', etc. that are alternative to M prove on balance as effective as M in conducing to the realization of μ.

Accordingly, one draws he conclusion that we are (relatively) justified in adopting M for the realization of μ.

Now it is clear that this line of argument is heavily laden with factual commitments, since the premises at issue in both items (2) and (3) represent a significant incursion into the realm of empirical fact. It is in principle impossible to attempt "the appeal to experience" regarding the "effectiveness in practice" or the "success in employment" of a method if we lack any and all data regarding the actual occasions of use of this or similar methods and the occurrences that followed thereupon. The generic structure of an instrumental justification of the experiential type requires us to recognize that have we adopted and implemented certain courses of action; to note that certain occurrences supervened upon these steps; and finally to assess these occurrences in point of their conduciveness to our objective μ. Putting the evaluative issues of this final item aside, we remark that the remaining points are entirely matters of record relating to past activities and observations. To implement the pragmatic program of determining whether a certain procedural method works out, we must inevitably have some informative *data regarding what was done and what happened*. It is self-evident that to apply any argument from experience we need factual records to tell us what experience has been.

We thus come to the crucial question: Given that factually informative data are needed for any application of the instrumental line of justification, just whence is one to obtain these factually informative historical inputs when this justification relates to our very criterion of factual truth itself? Clearly if the factual premisses are to come from the criterion C itself, then we move in the unhappy circle of invoking C to validate certain claims which claims are then in turn used for the validation of C.

If the experimentally pragmatic justification of a criterion C of factual truth is to succeed, this circle must be broken. But how are we to break it?

Only one way seems to be open. Insofar as they function as premiss-inputs into the justificatory argument for C, the experiential data must be seen *not as truths but merely as plausible presumptions*. We must distinguish the claim of *certainty* (a truth is, after all, in principle not defeasible—otherwise it would not be a truth) from the claim of *plausibility*. To class a proposition as *true* is (as John Dewey was wont to insist) very different from characterizing it as having some suitable degree of *warranted assertability*. From an epistemic standpoint there is a vast gulf between an established truth and a provisionally accepted supposition. There is a critical difference between characterizing a thesis as *prima facie* correct and acceptable in the first analysis (plausible or credible), and claiming it as ultimately correct and acceptable in the final analysis (actually true). To limit our purview to truths is to ignore that vast and important class of theses that are *tentatively* acceptable but subject to abandonment in the light of systematic considerations, and so ultimately defeasible.[3]

I have emphasized this distinction between genuine truths and merely presumptive truth-candidates at some length because it is crucial for present purposes. Any *experiential* justification of a

---

[3] This conception of data not as truths as such but merely as truth-candidates is elaborated in considerable detail in N. Rescher, *The Coherence Theory of Truth* (Oxford, The Clarendon Press, 1973).

truth-criterion must pull itself up by its own bootstraps. It needs factual inputs, but yet these factual inputs cannot at this stage already qualify as truths. To meet this need it is natural to appeal to truth-candidates, data which are no more truths than candidate-presidents are presidents—though some of them are ultimately bound to win out.

Accordingly, it is quite sufficient for our objective to have it that the retrospective record and memory yields informative yet infirm data, data of merely *prima facie* correctness that need not be ultimately true but are plausible truth-candidates. Not the outright *truth* but the mere *plausibility* of our retrospective records can provide the information-base needed for the pragmatic argument from experience. To be sure, it must be granted that only an argument from true premises can possibly *demonstrate* its conclusion. But this undoubted fact does not entail the (surely incorrect) consequences that arguments from merely plausible premises cannot carry substantial probative weight. Nothing untoward ensues from a recognition that our justificatory argument is presumptive rather than demonstrative in that some of its premises figure in the role of plausible data rather than certified truths.

7. POST HOC ERGO PROPTER HOC: A RESIDUAL CIRCULARITY

Yet another fundamental difficulty resides in the very nature of the premiss pivotal to any instrumentally teleological validation, namely the premiss to the effect

M works; i.e., employment of M is appropriately conducive to realization of the objective μ.

For when we take the experiential route to the establishment of this premiss, the only information we can obtain on the basis of the matters-of-historical-record (as dealt with in the preceding section) takes the following form:

(1) The method M has been tried (as have its alternatives M', M'', etc.).

(2) The objectives μ were realized sooner or more fully (more efficiently, more effectively) by M than in those cases where its competitors (M', M'', etc.) were employed.

So much can be available as a matter of historical record. But this will not suffice to establish the requisite degree of intimacy between the method M and the correlative desideratum μ. What is clearly needed to warrant the "is conducive" claim of the premiss is not just the *post hoc* information that M was adopted and the sought result μ achieved, but the *propter hoc* information that μ was attained because of the adoption of M. If the realization of μ is to validate M, then its *attributability to the use of M* must be established. To (1) and (2) above we must add

(3) In all (most) particular instances i: attainment of μ in instance i is attributable—or at least presumptively attributable—to the use of M.

That is, the thesis that "M works" must be regarded as a generalization of a host of specific cases of attribution to the use of M of instances of a successful realization of μ.

Now in general there is nothing in this state of affairs to create problems for a pragmatic validation. But in the specific cases of a criterion of truth C a serious difficulty crops up with respect to (3). For if our argument is to have proper probative weight, then all its premisses must be established, and while the matters of record at issue in (1)–(2) can be handled by the approach of the preceding section, the patently fact-claiming premiss (3), which is clearly *not* just a matter of historical record, poses altogether new difficulties. For any attempt to show that this attributability thesis (3) is true once again activates the specter of circularity: its truth will obviously be a matter of fact, but it is a criterion of factual truth we are endeavouring to validate. We seem once more to be plunged into the patently circular position that our validation of a criterion of factual truth calls for our *already* being in the possession of a validated factual truth.

The best resolution to this problem of validating a *propter hoc* attributability-claim is to see its appearance in the over-all justificatory argument not in the status of a *validated truth* at all (since this would indeed be circular), but rather in the status of a *warranted postulate*. Note that it does not even make sense to ask with respect to postulates (unlike theses, conjectures, assumptions, or hypotheses) whether they are true (*qua* postulates). With this approach we take the stance that when the *post hoc* facts are suitably adjusted—subject to all the appropriate controls and cautions of the theory of the design of experiments—then a certain postulation is warranted or justified.

Accordingly, we would adopt at the *regulative* level (rather than the factual or constitutive level) an operative precept of the type:

(P) To treat a certain *postulation* of propter-hocness as warranted under suitable circumstances regarding post-hocness.

This is itself a practical/procedural principle rather than a cognitive/factual thesis.[4] It indicates a mode of action rather than a claim to truth. Its status is methodological, and its validation is part and parcel of the overall program of instrumental validation we have taken into hand.[5]

It deserves note, incidentally, that its treatment as a justified postulate within the framework of the pragmatic argument does not preclude the prospect of *eventually* re-classifying an attributability thesis as a truth *ex post facto*, once the (duly justified) criterion *C* is itself applied. Nor indeed should one rule out the prospect that *in a particular instance*, a *propter hoc* attributability-contention should be ultimately classed as false by *C* (that *C* should, so to speak, on occasion bite the hand that feeds it).

On this line of approach, then, we start with the validating force of an operative precept of regulative status, affording us with a needful factual input whose standing is that of a warranted postulate rather than an established truth. Some such pre-

---

4 Regarding the process of imputation that underlies such a postulational attribution of propter-hocness on the basis of evidence relating to post-hoc relationships see Chapter III below, and also N. Rescher, *Conceptual Idealism* (Oxford, 1973).

5 However, the fact that in a case of this sort a *plurality* of principles comes concurrently into play gives to the over-all analysis a wholistic character whose implications are far-reaching. On the one hand, it means that when the justificatory principles P_1, P_2, . . ., P_n jointly lead to the correctness of the appropriate conclusion C, then the entire collection of principles P_1–P_n is supported at one stroke. But on the other hand if P_1, P_2, . . ., P_n fail to yield the appropriateness of C, then it becomes in principle impossible to pinpoint the specific sources of the difficulty in one of the P_i. Negative results are accordingly not very useful. The reader familiar with the discussion of Duhem's thesis in the recent literature of the philosophy of science will be able, *mutatis mutandis*, to apply the lessons of that problem to the present case.

C

justification-as-true warrant is clearly needed to avoid circularity in the justificatory argument. But nothing vicious ensues if it turns out from the *post-justificatory* standpoint—as indeed if all goes well it must, at least by-and-large—that the thesis whose *antecedent* status is a postulate should ultimately acquire the *consequent* status of a truth. And there is nothing fatal if in some instances the results of postulation turn out to be such that their consequent status is that of falsehood. A warranted postulate—unlike an established truth—is defeasible and can in the final analysis turn out to be untrue without thereby undoing its initial status as warranted. Its regulative acceptance does not render it incorrigible at the constitutive level.[6]

The logical structure of the justificatory process we have sketched looks as follows:

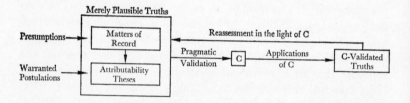

The over-all process envisages a feed-back loop leading from the C-validated truths back to the initial "merely presumptive" truths, so that the appropriateness of our means of obtaining the initial, tentative, merely plausible truths can be reassessed. Clearly if *most* of these were to turn out false in the light of C, something would have gone seriously amiss. The reasonableness of the over-all process thus rests on internal coherence and the mutual support that the various stages of the whole are able to lend to one another. The justificatory rationale must as a whole be coherent and self-sustaining.

[6] This conception of a pragmatically warranted postulate of essentially regulative import bears some points of resemblance to the theory of "fictions" developed in Hans Vaihinger's *Philosophy of 'As If'* (tr. C. K. Ogden, London, 1924). It would be false to claim Vaihinger as a precursor, since the similarity did not enter my mind until the present work was complete. But it would be unjust to fail to acknowledge the kinship of ideas, whose actual source is, simply enough, the common influence of Kant. (Cf. Chap. IV below.)

8. HUME'S PROBLEM

We come, finally, to the third seeming—and seemingly decisive —obstacle in the way of an experientially pragmatic justification of a criterion of truth, namely Hume's problem of the validation of reasoning from past to future.

To begin with, it is obvious that if one attempts any *experiential* justification of a truth-criterion, then one obtains a line of argument whose direction of motion is as follows:

C has provided truths $\to$ C provides truths in general

And plainly, this argument comprises *a fortiori* a subargument of the form:

C has provided truths $\to$ C will provide truths

Now it is clear by parity with our earlier reasoning that, quite apart from any special difficulties posed by Hume's problem, no justificatory reasoning of such a form can succeed with respect to a truth criterion (that is, to what really and truly in the final analysis is our truth criterion), because the essential premiss that C has provided truths is vacuous in having us judge the products of C by the circulatory trivializing standard of C itself.

But, of course, no comparable difficulty will affect the cognate inductive argument that proceeds on the practical (rather than theoretical) side, and has the aspect of the following line of reasoning:

C has provided satisfactory results $\to$ C provides satisfactory results in general

It is evident, however, that this reasoning would comprise *a fortiori* the sub-argument whose principal direction of motion is as follows:

C has provided satisfactory results $\to$ C will provide satisfactory results

And such an argument, while evading the previous obstacle of circularity, at once encounters Humean difficulties. For it seems that what is at issue here is still an *argument*, though now one of the *practical* form:

works in the past $\to$ works in the future

rather than the theoretical/cognitive form:

true in the past $\to$ true in the future

And it would seem that any such line of trans-temporal argument will at once run into the roadblock erected by Hume to preclude inferences regarding the future from premises relating to the past.

But any such discursive appearance is in reality misleading. For our actual concern here is not really at all with an *argument to establish a factual thesis* regarding the relationship of past and future occurrences—such as the regularity of nature—but with *the validation of a practice*: namely the implementation of the precept inherent in the following *practical* policy:

> To continue to use a method that has proven to be successful (i.e., more effective than alternatives) in those cases (of suitable numerousness and variety, etc.) where it has been tried.

The validation of this methodological precept lies deep in the nature of rationality itself, since it is quintessentially rational to continue to use for the attainment of specified objectives methods and procedures that have proven themselves effective in their realization.

The critical point is that in the context of our justificatory argument we are not dealing with the establishment of a factual thesis at all—be it demonstrative or presumptive—but merely with the rational validation of a practical course of action. And the practical warrant that rationalizes the use of a method need not call for a guarantee of success (which is, in the circumstances of the case in view, altogether impossible), but merely for having as good reasons as, under the circumstances, we can reasonably hope to have.

Of course, the issues that arise here are so more complex that these brief indications can do no more than point the way in the general direction of the proposed resolution. The next chapter will return to the matter in greater detail. But for present purposes, the important fact is that a promising avenue at least remains open for resolving this third seeming difficulty in the way of an experientially pragmatic justification of a criterion of factual truth.

9.   THE PRIMACY OF PRACTICAL REASON

The discussion has throughout proceeded on abstract and methodological plane; it has not sought to validate any *specific* criterion of truth, but has dealt solely with metacriteriological issues. All the same, some quite useful conclusions have, I think, emerged from these abstract deliberations.

Theoretical reason in the factual area moves towards a conclusion of the form ". . . is in fact the case regarding the world." Practical reason moves towards a conclusion of the form ". . . is to be done." With respect to the employment of a method it is clear that practical reason is the appropriate mode of justification, since the correctness of a method does not reside in its truth (methods and instrumentalities are by their very nature neither true nor false), but in its appropriateness (i.e., suitability to the task in view). And since the rational espousal of a factual truth must be governed by *some* appropriate criterion of acceptance, and any such a criterion is in effect methodological, it follows that in the factual domain practical reason is basic to the theoretical.

But how can the practical justification of a criterion C of factual truth proceed? Plainly by showing that "it works." But "it works" cannot here mean "succeeds in the theoretical/cognitive task of providing truths," which would commit a blatant circularity. Accordingly, "it works" is best and most apropriately to be construed as "works with the practical purpose of action-guidance." The range of affective purposes and man's material satisfactions is no less crucial for truths than the range of theoretical/cognitive purposes.

These considerations indicate that the ultimate metacriterial standard for weighing a criterion of truth-acceptance (in the factual area) is not *cognitive* at all, but rather *affective*, and the justificatory reasoning for the test-procedure of truth-determination represents in the final analysis an appeal not to knowledge, but to feeling. The affective dimension of *pain, frustration* of hope, *disappointment* of expectation—and their opposites—becomes the court of appeal that stands in ultimate judgment of our procedures for deciding upon questions of factual truth and falsity. In the final analysis cognition is ancillary to practice and *feeling* becomes the arbiter of empirical *knowledge*.

It is worthwhile to review in its generic outlines the whole line of reasoning that is at issue here. The components of a pragmatic validation of a truth-criterion that takes the route of an appeal to experience are as follows:

(1) A practical principle of regulative import is invoked to afford the plausibility (not truth) of matters of record.

(2) We note (as matters of record) that employment of the truth-criterion C has provided the C-validated propositions $p_1, p_2, \ldots$

(3) We note (as matters of record) that in various cases we acted upon these C-validated propositions.

(4) We note (as matters of record) that affectively advantageous results obtained in these cases—at least by and large.

(5) We note (as matters of record) that comparably advantageous results did not obtain in those cases where we acted upon criterion C', C'',..., that are alternative to C.

(6) A practical principle of regulative import is invoked to afford the plausibility (not truth) of the claim that the advantageous results that ensued upon the use of C were obtained *because* we employed C. Accordingly we attribute these results to C, and so obtain the essential premiss that "C works" in the pragmatic manner suitable for its methodological validation on grounds of "success."

(7) We then take the crucially pragmatic step of moving inferentially from the premiss that "C works" in this practical/affective sense to the conclusion of the (methodological) appropriateness of C, with the full range of wider implications that this carries with it.

Only with this last step—after invoking two practical principles and a great many presumptively factual claims—do we reach our final goal of experientially validating on pragmatic grounds the correctness of the truth-criterion C at issue.

It is crucially important to notice that this course of pragmatic validation is not in any direct way a pragmatic justification of the acceptance as true of some thesis or proposition. Rather it is a justification of a methodology, and its bearing on propositions is altogether indirect. A two-layer process is envisaged: the acceptance of a thesis as true is validated not in pragmatic terms at all, but in terms of the verdict of a criterion, but the appropriateness of this criterion is in its turn validated on pragmatic grounds.

The pivotal question is oviously this: How is one to argue that a criterion of factual truth "works" (from this pragmatic/

affective angle)? One can do so either on theoretical grounds of general principle (which are not available in any promising way) or on the basis of past experience. Now this recourse to the lessons of experience calls for two inputs: (1) information of the matter of record type, and (2) information regarding the attribution of results to procedures. Here the matters of record at issue must be seen not as *actual* (factual) truths, but as merely *presumptive* data. And the status of an attribution thesis must also be viewed as merely *presumptive* in that it represents a presumption based upon postulation. For undergirding this whole warranting process is an appeal to certain practical precepts of procedural justification that serves to define and constitute the very essence of rationality of action.

Accordingly, the experientially pragmatic justification of a criterion of factual truth does not constitute anything like a decisive demonstration. For the line of justificatory reasoning in view is based on defeasible presumptions as premises, and uses reasoning that is itself not demonstrative but merely plausible— in that it can be converted to demonstration only by the addition of presumption-based postulations. (The maintenance of a distinction between demonstration and plausible reasoning is crucial to the line of justificatory argumentation here.)

The experiential justification in view thus falls short of anything like a decisive demonstration. It does not and cannot *prove* that those criterial methods that have served us well in special cases must *in general* succeed better than alternatives. All the same, the practical reasoning in view is by no means devoid of the weight of rational warrant. It is unquestionably rational to change from what experience has marked as unsuccessful methods to experientially more favorable-seeming alternatives. To persist on a course or policy of action in the face of continual manifest failure and even disaster is, after all, the very quintessence of irrationality.

The experientially pragmatic validation of a criterion of factual truth is certainly called upon to resolve various serious difficulties in the way of its implementation. But it seems that it would be very ill-advised to take the reality of these, after all, not altogether insuperable difficulties as grounds for slamming the door on this justificatory approach. In view of the problems facing its alternatives, this experientially pragmatic route may well qualify, notwithstanding its inherent difficulties, as the most attractive strategy of criterial validation that is available to us in this matter of a criterion of factual truth.[7]

10. POSTSCRIPT: THE PROBLEM OF DETERMINATENESS

Any instrumental process for appraising the legitimizing warrant of a method (procedure, instrumentality, etc.) is inherently unable to provide a theoretical guarantee of a uniquely determinate solution. There is no general reason of principle why the means-to-ends appraisal of methods should issue in a single result; in general it is quite possible that different and distinct methods should be equally effective in realizing specified purposes. The instrumental strategy for assessing methods is accordingly potentially *under-determinative*: there can be no theoretical guarantee that one single result rather than a plurality of equally qualified ones will emerge from the analysis.

But this potential pluralism of the generic process of instrumental analysis does not preclude the specific circumstances of particular problem-areas from being such that a unique result can be expected *in this case* thanks to particular characteristics of the specific application at issue. Against this background it is worth noting that the particular application of instrumental validation that has concerned us here—viz., pragmatic procedures for validating methods governing the acceptance-as-true of factual theses—are indeed such as to militate towards a definiteness of result.

A postulate of rationality or reasonableness is an important part of the foundations of the line of justificatory reasoning in view: it is crucial that men not only hold beliefs as a kind of exercise in abstraction, but that our actions are in general guided by

[7] Historically, the doctrine of the primacy of practical over theoretical reason goes back to Schopenhauer's teaching that the intellect is altogether the servant of the will. The Schopenhaurian thesis that cognition is subordinate to the will is elaborated by R. H. Lotze and Christoph Sigwart (see the Introduction to Pt. III of his *Logic*, tr. by H. Dendy [London, 1895; orig. German ed. Leipzig, 1878]). From these writers the theory moves on the German side to neo-Kantian thinkers —such as Hans Vaihinger—who stress the prominence of practical reason, and on the American side through Peirce and James to the later pragmatists. (Note that James explicitly quotes Sigwart with approval.)

the beliefs we hold. Accordingly, our theorizing is not just of interest in itself (as part of a purely abstract quest for knowledge), but as providing the essential foundations of our practical and indeed survival-relevant activity. Theory must be determinative of action. If men were systematically passive (did not implement their beliefs in action) or perverse (acted counter to the indications of their beliefs), then the adequacy of their theorizing could obviously not be judged by its results. The acceptance of factual theses generally has extensive and immediate implications for action, and these actions produce results that reverberate back to their initiating agent in one way or another.

Both of these facets are important aspects of the metaphysical background: the *activism* of men in implementing their cognitive commitments, and the *sensitivity* of nature to human intervention (in the physics/engineering sense of this term), so that human agency produces a flow of consequences that rebound back upon the agent so as ultimately to produce success or frustration. If man were not highly activistic in implementing his beliefs about the nature of things, or if the world were such that these implementing actions were pretty much irrelevant to the course of things, the situation would be altogether different. If our beliefs did not issue in action and our actions did not produce a multitude of consequences measurable in terms of success or failure, then the discriminative "bite" of a policy of "awaiting nature's ruling" on the products of our methods of inquiry would be lost. Interaction and feedback are the key factors whose magnitude is bound to produce a substantial discriminative force in the testing of methods for validating factual views. Our validation of the primacy of practice and of the fundamental role of practical purposes as the controlling norms of theory in the epistemology of factual knowledge rest ultimately upon a metaphysical foundation whose supports are activism, interactionism, and feedback. And the discriminative power that is (presumably) inherent in these factors—and indeed amplified by the substantial degree of their presence—renders it *a priori* unlikely that substantially discordant fact-validating procedures would emerge from the analysis as to all appearances equally suitable.

On this line of thought, our theorizing is open to supportive evidence only when failure is risked, only if it is prepared to stub its toes on the hard rock of reality. (This in the final analysis is why the pragmatic validation of methods, though presumably effective in the sphere of our factual knowledge, is not comparably serviceable in the fields of metaphysics or theology.) If success is to be the touchstone of their validity, our methods of inquiry must actually be put to trial through an appeal to the court of experience.

The sceptical question remains:

But why is the pragmatic success of the deliverances to be taken to *justify* this criterion—i.e., to count towards establishing its "correctness" as a *truth* criterion?

This question is particularly problematic because " 'P' is true" certainly does not *mean* " 'P' is vouched for by pragmatically (or otherwise) successful criterion," but rather the meaning of "true" should continue to be understood in orthodox, correspondentist terms: " 'P' is true" iff P; that is, a true statement is one that affirms what is actually the case.

What validates the pragmatic account is not a definitional revisionism about the meaning of *truth*, but rather a certain *metaphysical* posture. This metaphysical stance runs as follows: that while action on false beliefs (i.e., those which fail to capture "what is actually the case") can on occasion succeed due to chance or good luck or kindly fate or whatever, the situation will be otherwise when it is not an isolated action or a particular belief that is at issue, but a general *policy* of acting, as based on a generic and methodologically universalized standard of belief-validation. When we view man as a vulnerable creature in close interaction with a hostile (or at best neutral) environment, it is conceivable that successful action on a false belief or even set of beliefs might be feasible, but it surpasses the bounds of plausibility to suppose that this could be so on a wholesale rather than retail basis. Given our assumptions of rationalism, activism, interactionism, feedback, sensitivity, and vulnerability it becomes statistically inconceivable that success should crown the products of *systematically* error-producing cognitive procedures. Perhaps ill luck might come in battalions rather than single spies, but with good luck the circumstances run in reverse.

Of course, the *results* of our duly justified truth-criterion must be such as to validate ultimately the system of these justificatory assumptions and presuppositions on which its validation rests.

This demand is simply another aspect of our earlier insistence upon the systematic coherence of the justificatory process as ultimately self-sustaining. (And I take it that in the present case there can be little question about the factual viability of the initial "metaphysical" stance on which the justificatory procedure rests.)

Accordingly, a sort of experientially Darwinian pragmatism is at issue here.[8] Theory is evaluated in terms of its guidance of action: theorizing canalizes our acts, leading to consequences of markedly practical implications, producing a feedback phenomenon that substantially affects our weal and woe. The correctness of such theorizing is presumptively reflected in its success in proving survival-conducive. The key presuppositions of the underlying justificatory process are rationality, activism, interactionism, and feedback. The fact that we are rational agents functioning in the environment of a duly responsive nature, and sensitively responsive to its operation, is crucial to the rationale of our methodologically pragmatic validation of the fundamentality of practical reason in the rational validation of our cognitive methodology.

Our analysis thus envisages a complex interdependence or symbiosis between our factual views and our practical objectives and so ultimately between the practical and the theoretical principles of rationality. Practical considerations serve to determine and to legitimate the methodological canons of our factual knowledge—just this is the burden of our primacy thesis. But, of course, to say this is not to deny that data validated as factual by such canons are inherently requisite in any reasoned pursuit of practical objective. (Without some recourse to purpose, facts are unattainable; without some recourse to facts, purposes are futile.) The complex dialectic of interaction and feedback between the practical and factual levels provides the forging heat by which our cognitive tools become hardened to the point where they support the scalpel's edge of scientific precision.[9]

[8] For further considerations regarding the pragmatic Darwinism with respect to conceptual schemes that is at issue here see Chapter IX ("Idealist Philosophy of Nature") of N. Rescher, *Conceptual Idealism* (Oxford, 1973).

[9] The discussion of this chapter offers an expanded reworking of material initially presented in Chap. X of N. Rescher, *The Coherence Theory of Truth* (Oxford, 1973).

Chapter II

A PRAGMATIC JUSTIFICATION OF INDUCTION

1. INTRODUCTION

In the preceding chapter the matter of the justification of induction was dealt with all too briefly as a side-issue in the course of other pursuits. To give the problem such relatively short shrift is evidently to do it the grave injustice of inadequate treatment. The present chapter seeks to atone for this defect by dealing with this issue in its own right and in greater detail. It will accordingly be the aim of this discussion to develop and advocate a justification of induction articulated along strictly pragmatic lines. Be it noted that "induction" is here to be construed generically to embrace any suitable rational process for the validation of an empirical generalization. Thus no substantial harm would ensue if one substitutes "scientific method" for "induction" throughout these pages.

The fundamental problem around which the discussion revolves is set by the following line of argument:

1. Every attempt to establish an empirical generalization by evidential means involves an implicit inference from past to future (because the evidence-in-hand must relate the past-cum-present, while any authentic empirical generalization will apply also to future cases).

2. Accordingly, an empirical generalization cannot be validated unless its implicit inferential move from facts about the past (which are at issue in the evidence) to claims about the future (which are implicit in the generalization itself) can be warranted.

3. An inferential move from past to future can be warranted only if it is shown that *nature is uniform* in the sense that there are fundamental stabilities in virtue of which those features nature has exhibited in the past will (at least by and large) continue to apply in the future.

4. The uniformity of nature is in principle not capable of being established: neither matters of *a priori* principle nor

matters of actual fact being available to warrant this claim.

Therefore, instantial evidence cannot provide a rational warrant for accepting an empirical generalization.

In this frame of reference, the basic problem is seen to be that of justifying claims about the future (as implicit in any generalization) in terms of facts about the past-cum-present (to which alone any available empirical evidence can possibly relate).

This Humean problem of justifying induction cuts to the very core of the problematic of scientific understanding and scientific rationality. If the scientific explanation of occurrences is to be possible, we must make use of suitably established generalizations. For scientific explanations are subsumptive arguments: they place the specific occurrences to be explained within the scope of covering-laws, as instances of generalizations that represent generic relationships. (Why did that ball drop X feet in the last minute? Because it was released at altitude from a state of rest into one of free fall and in the absence of resistance an object in free fall cover a distance $1/2$ gt^2.)

We thus face the results posed by the syllogism:

Any adequate scientific explanation calls for the use of validated empirical generalizations

No empirical generalization can be validated by our observational evidence

∴ There can be no adequate scientific explanation

The previous argument thus poses the threat of fundamental scepticism regarding the prospects of scientific rationalization of our understanding of the world.

It will be the task of the present chapter to maintain that the initially presented Humean argument rests on a defective premiss, namely the third one. Indeed I even propose to argue that, plausible appearances to the contrary notwithstanding, the validation of an empirical generalization does *not* require *a priori* warranting of past-to-future inferences, an upshot that would lead inevitably to presuppositions regarding the uniformity-of-nature.

2. THE METHODOLOGICAL PERSPECTIVE

It is undeniably *possible* to look upon an induction as an *argument*: a process of drawing a general conclusion of inherently future applicability from evidence regarding the past. But this admittedly *available* standpoint is not inevitable. And when we meet the Humean roadblock we do well to turn in another direction: it becomes desirable to see induction in an altogether different light.

The fundamental aim of induction is, after all, the validation of generalizations. Now to be sure, induction bases future-directed claims on past-directed evidence. But this is in fact irrelevant from the purposive aspect: the drawing of future-related claims from past-directed evidence may well describe the *procedure* of the enterprise, but is irrelevant to its *goals*. To regard the matter in this light of drawing inferences from past to future is to take an altogether misleading perspective.

The focal problem is not the specific issue of validating an inference from past to future, but that of supporting acceptance of a generalization. It is, of course, true, and *trivially* true, that any authentic *generalization* must apply to future cases—that "All leopards have spots" will envisage future leopards as well as past ones. And it is true, and *trivially* true, that all the *available* observational evidence must relate to the present or the past, since the future necessarily and in principle lies beyond the observational horizon. Unless one is to take the somewhat outrageous step of construing this combination of trivial truths as a decisive obstacle to the prospect of warranting the acceptance of a generalization, one has to recognize that an argument from past-oriented data to future-oriented claims is not the object of the enterprise. A time-spanning *inference* is simply not at issue. Rather, the fundamental task is just that of validating acceptance of a generalization.

Accordingly, induction comes to be seen in its *methodological* light as a procedure for providing a rational warrant for the acceptance of generalizations.

3. THE PRAGMATIC PERSPECTIVE

The mode of justification appropriate to anything *methodo-*

logical—a tool, procedure, instrumentality, program or policy of action, etc.—is inherent in the question: Does it work—that is, does it attain its intended purposes? Anything of methodological character is best validated in terms of its ability to achieve the purposes at issue; its success at accomplishing its proper task.

Applying these general—and virtually truistic—considerations to our specific case, we face the question of justifying induction in the following terms:

Does the inductive practice of basing empirical generalizations on the factual evidence of observations-in-hand actually work?

Observe the dual aspect of justification that follows from viewing the matter at a methodological level. (1) We justify a *thesis* (empirical generalization) in terms of the method (practice) that produces it, viz., the scientific method. (2) We justify the *method* in terms of its success ("it works"). The crux of our approach is thus to combine a methodological justification of substantive *theses* with a practical or instrumental justification of regulative *methods*. Such a Kantian distinction between constitutive and regulative considerations provides the pivot around which the course of argumentation is to turn.

But first off we must face the critical problem of what "it works" means in the setting of such an instrumental validation, and—above all—how this "it works" is to be established in the case at hand.

Of course, an evidentially falsified or disconfirmed generalization must be ruled out, but this step does not take us far. The absence of evidential invalidation is no touchstone of truth—as any statistician knows from curve-fitting problems, *mutually* incompatible generalizations may yet be compatible with all the evidence. Where generalizations are concerned, finite evidence cannot go as far as to yield assured truth, and so the "it works" at issue cannot mean success at providing correct (true) empirical generalizations.

Since the test of success cannot in principle lie in the provision of recognizably *true* generalizations, we do well to explore the prospects of the pragmatists' transformation of "success" from *cognitive* success to *practical* success, to working out as a guide of action. (Of course, a *part* of this working-out can be construed in factual rather than pragmatic terms—e.g., systematic consistency with other generalization and consonance with "established fact." But the significance of *these* factual conditions is wholly negative—in defining a class of eligible, noneliminated cases— and is thus overshadowed by that of the pragmatic factors now at issue.)

Our acceptance or nonacceptance of generalizations, of course, has extensive involvements on both the cognitive and the affective sides of the theoretical/practical divide, since such acceptance is a guide both as to belief and as to action. And the propositions we accept as true yield both information about the world and guidance for action, with the correlated sanctions of error in the intellectual, and pain (frustration, etc.) in the practical areas. Hence any process for validating the acceptance of generalizations comes to be endowed with a duality of objectives: on the one hand as a standard of belief in purely intellectual regards, and on the other as a guide for our practical life.

The structure of the problem is as follows: One begins with some proposed procedure for validating a generalization. The task is then that of showing that adoption of this procedure is successful in practice. Here "successful practice" should, as we have already argued, be construed to exclude purely *epistemic* practice of knowledge-acquisition and may address itself substantially to considerations of actual *activity-oriented* practice: action-guidance as assessed in the affective order of leading to physically and emotionally satisfying results (no pain, frustration of plans, unpleasant shocks, etc.). Our instrumentalism at this point takes a specifically pragmatic turn.

But the fundamental difficulty of reasoning from past to future now comes upon us again, albeit from a different direction. For the practical "it works" that is in view must be construed to mean "works *in general.*" We must accordingly face the problem of how this is to be established, given that our evidence for this general claim must itself relate to the past-cum-present.

We thus return from a different (for now *practical*) direction to Hume's problem of the validation of reasoning from past to future. And this fact appears to create a seemingly decisive obstacle in the way of an experientially pragmatic justification of induction.

4. SIDESTEPPING HUME'S OBSTACLE

On first sight it would seem that what is at issue in our pragmatic justification is still an *argument*, though one of the *practical* form

works in the past → works in the future

rather than the theoretical/cognitive form

true in the past → true in the future

Any such line of argument will run into the roadblock erected by Hume to preclude inferences regarding the future from premisses relating to the past.

But as already noted, this discursive appearance is misleading. For our actual concern here is once again simply with implementing the precept inherent in the following practical policy:

> To continue in the absence of countervailing considerations—of specific rather than generically sceptical bearing—to use a method that has proven to be successful (i.e., more effective than alternatives) in those analogous cases (of suitable numerousness and variety, etc.) where it has been tried.

An objector will complain: "But you cannot vindicate a policy by just *saying* it is rational, you have to *show* that it is rational. That is, you must point to something about it that *makes* it rational." So be it. The consideration that rationalizes the policy of continuing, in the absence of any specific indications to the contrary, the use of a method (procedure) that has succeeded is just this very fact of established success itself. Of course, success in the past does not *guarantee* continued success. But the very fact that it has proven effective in certain cases is, after all, *some reason*—however inconclusive—for thinking that the procedure may work in general: instances of success do carry *some* evidential weight in point of general efficacy—however little it may be. And if there is no reason at all to think that any other method that lies to hand will do better, then we do, after all, have adequate rational warrant for continued use of the method.

It is altogether crucial for the present line of reasoning to keep in mind our division of labour into the methodological validation of factual *theses* and the pragmatic validation of epistemic *methods*. The issue is at bottom the *regulative* one of practices for proceeding in the *constituting* of our factual knowledge, rather

D

than one of the substantive content of the specific factual claims or theses of which our knowledge is *constituted*.

But does the rational warranting of a practice not demand the establishment of the corresponding thesis?

No—not at all. The argument in support of a practice need not take the form of showing that this practice will in fact prove successful. It is a false claim that a practice is rationally warranted only if one somehow establishes that it *will* work. Rather, a practice is rationally warranted when it can be shown it *may* work and there is no reason to think that an alternative method affords a better promise of success. The fundamentally instrumental aspect of this line of argumentation warrants emphasis. Accordingly, our warrant for adopting a method need not reside in any demonstration of the thesis that applications of the method must prove successful in the attainment of its objectives. All we obtain and *all we need* is a more modest basis of establishing that there is somehow present, within the over-all epistemic structure of the situation, *some sort* of appropriate rational justification for the use of a method. And precisely because an appropriate provision of rational warrant can take the practical rather than theoretical route, an instrumental justification need not, at the methodological level, attempt the sort of theoretical guarantee of success inherent in arguments for the regularity of nature, or other tempting steps that collide outright with Hume's barrier.

5. PRACTICAL PRECEPTS VS. FACTUAL THESES

The critical point is that this justificatory strategy does not address itself to the establishment of a factual thesis at all—be it demonstrative or presumptive—rather, what we are dealing with is the rational validation of a practical course of action. Now it is important to recognize two very different constructions of the validation of the rational acceptability of the "it works" claim that is at issue:

As a thesis: establishing the factual contention that what works in the past will work in the future

As a practical precept: legitimating the practical step of using in the future those methods (practices, instrumentalities, etc.) that have worked in the past.

Crucial differences obtain here: proving a thesis is a very different sort of thing from warranting a practice. On the methodological perspective, the pivotal issue is not the *factual* one of establishing an empirical generalization, but rather that of legitimating an operational program of action. The objective at *this* level of discussion is not establishing the truth of a generalization but validating the rationality of a practice (an *epistemic* practice, to be sure, by which generalizations are supported).

The over-all structure of the reasoning is admittedly such that the inferential move

$$\text{past} \to \text{future}$$

does eventually get validated. And someone can object: "If you are to vindicate

$$\text{instance} \to \text{generalization}$$

then you must first validate its component

$$\text{past} \to \text{future}$$

since the former line of reasoning contains this as an *a fortiori* component." But this objection confuses logical prerequisites with probative ones. The fact that A entails B, does not mean that we cannot demonstrate A without "first" demonstrating B. Consider an entailment of the pattern

a certain specific X has $P \to$ something-or-other has P

An instance would be as follows:

triangles have a sum of interior angles amounting to $180° \to$
  equilateral triangles have . . .

Because the entailing antecedent "requires" the entailed consequent in the *logical* order, does not mean that we cannot give priority to this antecedent in the *probative* order of supportive reasoning.

But now the following further objection may well be made: "This practical line of approach could not do its justificatory task if facts about *working* in the past are devoid of evidential weight vis-à-vis success in the future. And why should *past* success count as proper evidence for success in the future?" We reply: To take the past-to-future perspective is to pick up the wrong end of the stick. The crucial issue is simply and atemporally: Why should a method's having *some* success count as evidence towards its promise of proving successful in general?

The answer to this pivotal question lies in a fundamentally this-or-nothing argument:

> If you are prepared to let *anything* in the line of available information count as evidence for a practical precept of the ϕ-works-in-general type (that is, if in this practical context you are going to play the rationality game of giving evidence and reasons at all), then you simply have no alternative to letting ϕ-works-in-some-cases count, because it is true *as a matter of principle* that in the case of a practice, method, or procedure rooted in the contingent sphere of empirical fact this is the only sort of "evidence" of suitability that one can ever hope to have in hand.

A this-or-nothing argument of this sort can provide the basis for validating the step of giving at least *some* evidential weight to the experiential data in such practice-justifying cases.

When we continue to use a method that succeeds, we implement a certain practical precept of action. Its legitimation does not reside in the fact that adherence to this precept cannot possibly fail us. Rather, our justification inheres in the fact that this step is rational because it's the best we can do under the circumstances. For we must accept the blunt impact of the following argument:

1. We need *some* evidence to validate the rational espousal of a practice.
2. The only appropriate kind of *available* evidence regarding the merits of a practice relating to factual issues is experiential: how it has fared in a range of previous trials.
3. Experiential evidence-in-hand must be of the observation-to-date type, and so must relate to the past-or-present.

∴ We must let the evidence of established performance count in legitimating any factually oriented practice.

To be sure, its experiential support through evidence-in-hand regarding its record of success does not *prove* that a method will succeed in future applications. But the probative weight of experience cannot be altogether discounted: established success must be allowed to carry *some* weight. A tried and successful method is "in possession of the field" as it were. A successful method cannot properly be treated with unqualified sceptical contempt. To be sure, established success is no *proof* of further efficacy, but in the face of established success the *burden* of proof shifts. *Initially* the proper question may have been "Why should we think the method works in this case?", but in the face of established success the question becomes: "Given its successful use in the past, why *shouldn't* we think the method will succeed?" The rationality of the practical sphere is such that given a record of past success on the part of a method, the natural presumption is now in its favour. The crucial point is that the "it works" at issue in the practical precept is not "it always does work" (as a thesis) but derives from a dialectic of rationality linked to the construction that

> "it works"=it works insofar as the only evidence we can hope to gather to show, i.e., as far as our relevant data can possibly reveal.

We thus arrive at the following line of thought:

(1)   The justification of method is seen as forthcoming in *practical* and not *substantive* terms ("it works" NOT "it is correct").

(2)   We view induction (scientific method) as a *method* for establishing generalizations.

(3)   A practical justification is then obtained on *experiential* grounds. The fact that experience relates to past-or-present is seen as *inevitable* and accordingly cuts no ice against basing future-committed claims on it.

The legitimation at issue in this course of justification is thus not the rationality of demonstrating a thesis (uniformity of nature), but that of validating a practice which is then in turn thesis-warranting.

6.   THE STRUCTURE OF OUR ARGUMENTATION

It is worthwhile in the interests of precision to set out in detail the structure of the preceding validation of the quasi-inferential move from past to future inherent in an inductive generalization:

(A)   *A pragmatic justification of the continued use of a success-ful method of practice.* The argument here goes essentially as follows:
  1. There is *some* reason to think the method will work.
  2. There is no reason to think that an alternative method will work better.

∴ We are justified in using the method in view.

(B)   *A this-or-nothing validation for according some probative weight towards the claim that a method works to its record of past success.* This proceeds along the following lines:
  1. If we do not count past instances of its success as having at least *some* tendency to show that a method for establishing fact-purporting generalizations will work, then we can never obtain any supportive warrant for this claim.
  2. It is unreasonable to preclude any and every empirical data from having a least some weight (however diminutive) towards the warranting support of a method.

∴ We are justified in counting the record of past successes as having at least some weight in warranting a method (as being one that works in general).

(C)   We combine (A) and (B) in arguing that *induction is a practice whose continued employment is warranted in the light of its past successes.*

This outline indicates the first cycle of the argument: the validation of induction as a practice.

We first validate a generalization (not pragmatically at all, but) as a product of induction as an independently validated methodology. And we thereupon invoke the generalization as supporting a move from the data of the past (in the supporting evidence from this generalization) towards the applications relating to future cases which that generalization admits.

The structure of the argumentation thus takes the following form:

(1) Methodological validation of induction as a practice.
(2) Inductive validation of a particular generalization on the basis of past-related data.
(3) Essentially *deductive* application of the generalization with respect to future exemplifications.

On this line of reasoning, it becomes clear that an argument of the form

past → future

is never used as an inferential step in the course of reasoning. At the level of stage (2) we take the inductively evidential step:

past-related evidence → generalization

and thereupon at the level of stage (3) we take the applicatively inferential step:

generalization → future-related instantiation

But because our over-all argument requires combining these two stages, we cannot here take "Carnap's shortcut" and move directly from past cases to future cases without the intervention of a generalization.[1] In fact, the intervening role of a generalization is seen as *crucial* to the rational validation through the route of practical considerations ("our inductive practices").

Fundamentally, the issue is thus not at all one of validating an *inference* from past to future, but rather of validating a *practice* for establishing a generalization—a practice that places the locus of evidence for generalizations into the orbit of cases-in-hand. No *inference* at all is operative here. No rational guarantee is offered or demanded.

The foundations of empirical generalization are thus seen to be themselves regulative, and not constitutive. A thesis is validated through a method, which method is in its turn justified by the pragmatic route. The basic move of this argumentation is reductive: it carries *validating a generalization* back to *validating a practice*. Not the truth of a generalization, but the rationality of a practice becomes the ultimate issue.

7. THE PRIMACY OF PRACTICAL REASON

Some writers have sought to support induction on the grounds that it represents the *natural* method of generalization-validation

---

[1] Cf. Rudolf Carnap, *Logical Foundations of Probability* (Chicago, 1950; 2nd ed., 1962), sect. 110, Appendix H.

that is appropriate to our verification procedures in science and common life, and that answers the demands of common sense. This approach is not adequate to the philosophical needs of the situation, for seemingly natural and common-sense procedures are not rationally justified by their possession of these features of naturalness. It is in their suitability to common-sense *aims*—not their conformity to common sense *methods*—that we see the validation of our inductive practices. And this points to the fundamentally pragmatic nature of our approach.

The justification of induction is accordingly seen as ultimately pragmatic. It is crucial to note, however, that the pragmatic test is here applied not to *individual* generalizations as a test of *truth*, but to a generic *method*-for-validating-generalizations as an appropriate *course of procedure*. A two-layer process is at issue: *generalizations* themselves are validated with reference to methods, and only these methods in turn are justified with reference to the pragmatic considerations of success in rational systematization and in practical action.

Our pragmatism here is again of the second order: *theses* are viewed as warranted unpragmatically by *methods*, and methods in turn as warranted pragmatically by results. Two distinct justificatory stages are at issue, only the second of which is pragmatic in character. The case is analogous to act vs. rule utilitarianism in ethics. The rule utilitarian wants to justify actions with reference to rules, these rules themselves alone being supported by utilitarian considerations. The distinction between the *proposition-pragmatism* of the Jamesian variety and our own *method-pragmatism* is exactly parallel to this. The *methodological* pragmatism here at issue is concerned with the pragmatic legitimation of generic methods; it is not a *substantive* pragmatism that seeks the establishment of specific theses or propositions about what goes on in the world.

On this approach *practice* is the arbiter of theory. And in place of a Kantian aprioristic "deduction" of our inductive practices, their present legitimation takes the form of an epistemic pragmatism. *Pragmatism* enters in because we seek validation in the assessment of "what works out"; and it is an epistemic version of this approach because methods for the acquisition of information are at issue. In the final analysis, the validation of our inductive practices is seen to lie not in their demonstrative success in furnishing truths (which, since *general* truths are at issue, they could not in principle do), but in their providing the instruments by which we can effectively manage our practical affairs and successfully find our way about within the realm of nature.[2]

8. AN OBJECTION

An objection to this mode of procedure remains to be dealt with, one that can be formulated as follows:

> If our only concern were to persuade people *already* using induction that there is nothing unreasonable in their practice, then the proposed pragmatic legitimation might be adequate. But surely the task goes beyond this. We should establish not just that it is reasonable for its adherents to continue using induction, but that any other way of forming expectations about the as-yet-unknown is in principle unreasonable, and that people using different methods are inevitably in an untenable position.

This objection asks for more than our line of argument affords, but in doing so it asks too much. Our justificatory reasoning relied upon the argument:

There is some reason to think method M will work.
There is no reason to think that any alternative method will work better.

∴ We are justified in using the method M.

Now to obtain the second premiss of this argument it would suffice to secure the auxiliary premiss:

(A) There is good reason to think that no *proposed* alternative method will work better.

But to establish—as the objection demands—the conclusion that "M is the *only* method whose use is justified" we would have to obtain not just (A), but

---

[2] For a development of these points see Pt. III of author's *Scientific Explanation* (New York, 1970)—from which the substance of the preceding two or three paragraphs has been drawn—as well as parts of Section 9 below.

(B) There is good reason to think that no *possible* alternative
method will work (at all).

But it is clear—if only owing to the change from *proposed* to
possible (and for the present ignoring that from "work better" to
"work at all")—that this second premiss could never possibly be
established in the present case of methods for validating empirical claims. The *in principle* inaccessibility of this needed premiss renders the demand implicit in the initial objection an
inherently unreasonable one, and underwrites the appropriateness
of our (admittedly weaker) mode of validation.

The pragmatic approach is in a position to deal with the
concrete proposal of *specific* alternatives to induction (≅scientific
method), since here its strategy of "the proof of the pudding is in
the eating" can apply. It cannot refute at the theoretical level
the generic thesis that some *possible* alternative to induction might
prove superior. But, given that we are dealing with *methods* rather
than *theses* (so that the *onus probandi* lies on the favourable
side), nothing is seriously put at risk by this incapacity at the
theoretical level to provide something which *in the very nature
of the case* is not to be had, and whose requirement is thus
inherently unreasonable.

9.   RATIONAL DARWINISM AS A PRAGMATIC BASIS
OF LEGITIMACY

The crucial question of the sources of rational warrant for the
standard inductivist practices remains to be dealt with more
explicitly.

The critical step is to recognize that the question "Why do our
conceptual methods and mechanisms fit 'the real world' with
which we interact intellectually?" simply does not permit of any
strictly aprioristic answer in terms of purely theoretical grounds of
general principle. Rather, it is to be answered in basically the
same way as the question: "Why do our bodily processes and
mechanisms fit the world with which we interact physically?"
Both are alike to be resolved in essentially evolutionary terms.

The standard conceptual machinery for structuring our view
of reality, our categorial perspective upon things and the intellectual mechanisms by which we form our view of "the way the

world works" are built up by an historic, evolutionary process in terms of "trial and error"—exactly as with the bodily mechanisms by which we comport ourselves in the physical world. These procedures accordingly develop subject to revision in terms of "success and failure" subject to standards themselves defined by the norms of the enterprise of rational inquiry. The concept of a "governing purpose" here serves as a regulative guide, exactly as in any other goal-oriented human activity.

It is important to understand that, when we speak here of "methods" for validating explanations, it is *discursive and explanatory methods* that are specifically at issue. That is why an appeal to authority (for example) does not constitute a method of the sort at issue. No matter how sucessful it might be in providing right answers, it does not provide these answers in the right sort of way, since its results are mere "givens" wholly devoid of explanatory rationalization.

As with any tool or instrument, the question of evaluation takes the form of a pragmatic assessment: Does it work? Does it produce the desired results? Is it successful in practice? The central issue is a matter of "survival of the fittest" with *fitness* assessed in terms of the practical objectives of the rational enterprise. Legitimation is found in substantial part in the fact of survival through historical vicissitudes. This subordination of theory to practice in the domain of rationality as understood in the Western tradition derived from the Greeks points to a *pragmatic* aspect of the theory which must be analyzed in detail. The pivotal issue is that of working out best.

But what does "best" mean here? This carries us back to the Darwinian perspective. A Darwinian legitimation clearly requires a standard of "fitness." There are a *variety* of conceptual schemes regarding "how things work in the world." The examples of such occult explanatory frameworks as those of numerology (with its benign ratios), astrology (with its astral influences), and black magic (with its mystic forces) indicate that there are alternative explanatory frameworks, and that these can have diverse degrees of merit. The governing standards of the Western tradition of human rationality are presented by the goals of *explanation*, *prediction*, and control. (And thus not, for example, sentimental "at-oneness with nature." Thus think of the magician vs. the mystic vs. the sage as cultural ideal.) I have taken the position here that this standard is provided by considerations of *practice* and is inherent in the use to which conceptual schemes are put in the conduct of our affairs. In the Western intellectual tradition the ultimate standards of rationality are defined by a very basic concept of knowledge-wed-to-practice, and their ultimate validation lies in the combination of theoretical and practical *success*: i.e., success of theory in the effective guidance of action.

Of course the pivotal issue is *survivability* and not mere *survival*. Admittedly, this Darwinian line of methodological justification can be effective only with respect to a culture which (as is the case with that of Western civilization) is highly *activistic* in its life-style, that is, which has a high density of interactions with the natural environment. If frustration (pain, etc.) is to serve as a basis for the rejection of procedures, methods (etc.), then the opportunity for such frustration must obtain. The survival at issue must not simply be a matter of a lucky fluke or a happy accident.[3] The belief-validating methods of a fortunate primitive tribe on an idyllic south sea island may survive for millenia without this fact constituting a substantial support of their adequacy. The circumstances of the case must be such that the fact of survival provides appropriate evidence for survivability—that is, yields an adequate basis of rational warrant for the postulation of a claim to survival-conducive characteristics. Only if this condition is met does Darwinian survival constitute evidence for pragmatic efficacy (i.e., shows that conditions for the premiss "it works" are satisfied in an appropriate way). But when this condition is (presumptively) met, then the Darwinian approach does endow the realities of actual practice and "the fact of possession" with probative weight, at any rate where methods (rather than beliefs, for example) are at issue.

10.   A REBUTTAL OF SCEPTICISM

This line of thought indicates how our inductive practices can be secured against the assault of traditional philosophic scepticism. In one classical form, the sceptic's argument goes as follows: "The rational man must, of course, have a basis for his beliefs and opinions. Thus, asked *why* he accepts some accepted belief or

---

[3] This is why we cannot simply apply to methods the Hegelian precept that *die Weltgeschichte ist das Weltgericht.*

opinion, he will cite one (or more) others that support it. But we can now ask him why he accepts these in turn, and this process can be continued as long as one likes. As a result, we will either move in a circle—and so ultimately provide no justification at all—or became involved in an infinite regress, supporting the elephant on the back of a turtle on the back of an alligator, etc. The only way to terminate the regress is by a dogmatic acceptance, somewhere along the line, of an *ultimate* belief that is used to justify others but is not itself justified. But any such unjustified acceptance is by its very nature arbitrary and irrational." So reasons the philosophic sceptic.[4]

The answer to this line of scepticism lies in recognizing that the things one rationally accepts are not of a piece. Specifically, it is necessary to give a careful heed to the essentially Kantian distinction between substantiative *theses* on the one hand and regulatve *methods* on the other. It is indeed ultimately unsatisfactory to adopt the purely discursive course of justifying theses in terms of further theses in terms of further theses, etc. But reflection on the rational legitimation of the scientific enterprise shows that this is not at all the issue here. Rather, we justify our acceptance of certain theses because (ultimately) they are validated by the employment of a certain method, the scientific method, thus breaking outside the cycle of justifying thesis by thesis through the fact that a thesis can be justified by application of a method. And we justify the adoption of this method in terms of certain *practical* criteria: success in prediction and efficacy in control. Our dialectic of justification thus breaks out of the restrictive confines of the sceptic's circle, and does so without relapse into a dogmatism of unjustified ultimates. We justify the aceptance of theses by reference to the method from which they derive, and we justify the method in terms of the classical pragmatic criterion of methodological validation. (With respect to *methodology*, at

---

[4] Considerations along these lines have led various recent epistemologists of the *foundationalist* tradition (as it might be called) to give up all prospects of "knowledge" in the sense of rationally-validated-acceptance-as-true. Exactly this is the position of Rudolf Carnap with respect to empirical generalizations (see his *Foundations of Probability*, *op. cit.*, Appendix H). Cf. also the more radical position of Keith Lehrer, "Why Not Scepticism?", *The Philosophical Forum*, vol. 2 (1971), pp. 283–98, as well as Peter Unger, "A Defense of Skepticism," *The Philosophical Review*, vol. 80 (1971), pp. 198–219.

any rate, the pragmatists were surely in the right—there is certainly no better way of justifying a *method* than by establishing that "it works" with respect to the specific tasks held in view.) The line of approach adopted here thus blocks this route towards philosophical scepticism by a complex, two-stage maneuver, combining the methodological justification of induced *theses* with the pragmatic justification of the inductive *method*.

Chapter III

THE IMPUTATIONAL THEORY OF LAWS

1. WHAT IS A UNIVERSAL LAW? THE NATURE OF LAWFULNESS

Scientific explanations of the circumstances and occurrences of nature are subsumptive arguments: they place particular events and states of affairs as special cases within a systematic framework of order delineated through laws.[1] Our standard concept of explanation—causal explanation preeminently included—is such as to require that the generalizations used for explanatory purposes must be of a special sort: they must be *lawful.* And clearly, not just any universal empirical generalizations will qualify as a law in this scientific context of discussion—no matter how well established it may be. It is critically important to distinguish here between *accidentally* true generalizations on the one hand and *lawful* generalizations on the other. "All coins in my pocket weigh less than one ounce" and "All American presidents are natives of the *continental* United States" are examples of accidentally true generalizations. By contrast, generalizations like "All elm trees are deciduous," "All (pure) water freezes at $32°F$" and "All Y-chromosomes self-duplicate under suitable stimulation" are lawful. A (potentially accidental) generalization can as such claim merely that something *is* so, perhaps even that it *is always* so; a lawful generalization goes beyond such a merely *de facto* claim to stipulate that something *must* (in some appropriate sense) be so.

Thus consider the following two explanatory answers to the question: "Why did that tree shed its leaves last fall?"

(1) Because it is an elm, and *all elms are deciduous.*
(2) Because it is a tree on Smith's property, and *all trees on Smith's property are deciduous.*

The drastic difference in the satisfactoriness of these two "explan-

---

[1] The analysis of explanation and lawfulness given in this chapter was initially presented in the author's *Scientific Explanation* (New York, 1970), and subsequently in a more developed form in *Conceptual Idealism* (Oxford, 1973). The present discussion draws upon the treatment given in these books, to which the reader is referred for a more extensive treatment of the author's views on this issue.

ations" is due exactly to the fact that the generalization deployed in the first case is lawful, whereas that in the second is not.

Natural laws are akin to but significantly different from both rules and descriptions. Like rules, laws tell us how things "must be," yet unlike most familiar rules laws admit no exceptions, but are always and inevitably "obeyed." Like descriptions, laws state how things are; yet unlike standard descriptions, laws go beyond describing how things in fact *are* to make claims about how they *must be*. Thus laws are akin both to descriptive characterizations and to norms; they have both a descriptive and a rulish side that prevents their being grouped squarely into either category. And the necessitarian aspect inherent in their rulishness is the essential feature that marks them as genuine laws.[2]

But just what is this factor of lawfulness present with respect to some generalizations and absent with others? The best way to answer this question of what lawfulness *is* is by inquiring into what it *does*. Lawfulness manifests itself in two related ways: *nomic necessity* and *hypothetical force*. Nomic necessity represents the element of *must*, of inevitability. In asserting it *as a law* that "All A's are B's" ("All timber wolves are carnivorous") we claim that *it is necessary* the world being as it is, that an A will be a B (i.e., that a timber wolf will under appropriate circumstances unfailingly develop as a meat-eating animal).

This nomic necessity manifests itself most strikingly in the context of hypothetical suppositions—with counterfactual hypotheses especially. In accepting the contention that "All A's are B's" ("All spiders are eight-legged") *as a law*, we have to be prepared to accept the conditional "If x were an A, then x would be a B." ("If this beetle were a spider [which it is not], then it would have eight legs." "If the [nonexistent] animal I'm thinking of were a [real] spider, then it would have eight legs.")[3] It is

<hr>

[2] This nomological necessity of laws is generally called "nomic necessity," following W. E. Johnson, *Logic, Part III* (Cambridge, 1924), p. 9. Cf. J. M. Keynes, *A Treatise on Probability* (London, 1921), pp. 251, 263, where Keynes speaks (*pace* Hume) of the lawfulness of general uniformity as involving a "necessary connection."

[3] The double example has a point: the x of the formula ranges over existents and nonexistents alike. In the former case (when we assume an actually existing thing to be different) we have a *modificatory counterfactual* conditional whose antecedent negates some actual fact. ("If this

preeminently this element of hypothetical force that distinguishes a genuinely lawful generalization from an accidental generalization like "All coins in my pocket weigh less than one half ounce." For we would not be prepared to accept the conditional "If a Venetian florin were in my pocket, then it would weigh less than one half ounce."[4] The critical difference between a merely factual (and so potentially accidental) generalization and an authentically lawful one does not reside in the reference to a limited period of time (why could a law not obtain during one transient cosmic era?). Rather the critical aspect of a law lies in the force of necessity it carries. And on this, surely most plausible, conception of lawfulness there is no reason of principle why a genuinely lawful relationship could not obtain with respect to one particular thing (the magnetic north pole or the Van Allen radiation belt) or one particular spatio-temporal region (a black hole).

The fact is that the statement:

(I) All X's are Y's

makes a stronger claim when put forward as a law than when put forward as a "mere" generalization. For if (I) is construed as a law, then it asserts "All X's have to be Y's," and so we obtain the stronger nomological generalization:

(II) All X's are Y's *and further* if any z that is not an X were an X, then z would be a Y.[5]

---

dog in the room were an elephant [which it isn't], then . . .") In the second case (when the thing at issue is nonexistent) we have a *speculative* counter-factual. ("If there were an elephant in the room [which there isn't], then. . . .") The former type *changes* the things of this actual world, the latter type makes additions to (or subtractions from) them. It will not be without significance for our subsequent argument that laws support counterfactuals of both the thing-modifying and the thing-introducing varieties.

4 It is clear that we mean this to be construed as "if it were somehow *added to* the coins in my pocket" and not as "if it were to be somehow *identical with* one of the coins in my pocket."

5 Roderick M. Chisholm has put this point with admirable precision: Both law statements and non-law statements may be expressed in the general form, "For every *x*, if *x* is an S, *x* is a P." Law statements unlike non-law statements, seem, however, to warrant inference to statements of the form, "If *a*, which is not S, were S, *a* would be P" and "For every *x*, if *x* were S, *x* would be P." R. M. Chisholm, "Law Statements and Counterfactual Inference," *Analysis*, vol. 15 (1955), p. 97.

E

When a generalization is taken as lawful it obtains added force: it gains a further assertive increment—even though this nomic necessity may well express itself primarily in applications of a counterfactual or fictional kind. It is in the conceptual nature of things that nomic necessity manifests itself most strikingly in such hypothetical and counterfactual contexts.[6]

To clarify this nomic-necessity aspect of lawfulness, let us consider the counterfactual supposition: *Assume that this wire (which is actually made of copper) were made of rubber.* This supposition occurs in the following context:

Items of Knowledge
    Facts: (1) This wire is made of copper.
           (2) This wire is not made of rubber.
           (3) This wire conducts electricity.
    Laws: (4) Copper conducts electricity.
           (5) Rubber does not conduct electricity.
    Hypothesis: Not-(2), i.e., This wire is made of rubber.

To restore consistency in our knowledge in the face of this hypothesis we must obviously give up (1) and (2). But this is not sufficient. One of (5) or (3) must also go, so that *prima facie* we could adopt either of the conditionals:

(A) If this (copper) wire were made of rubber then it would not conduct electricity (because rubber does not conduct electricity).

(B) If this (copper) wire were made of rubber, then rubber would conduct electricity (because this wire conducts electricity).

That is, we get a choice between retaining (5) with alternative (A) and retaining (3) with alternative (B). In classing a generali-

---

[6] Of course, strictly factual statements can also underwrite counterfactuals. From "Mr. X has property φ" it (presumably) follows that "If Mr. Y were Mr. X, he would have property φ." But note that it is a relationship of *identity* that is at issue here. When I use the law "copper conducts electricity" to infer "If this stick were copper, it would conduct electricity," this is not to be construed in identity terms as "If this stick were to be identical with one of the existing copper objects it would conduct electricity," but rather as "If this stick were somehow added to the existing copper objects, it would conduct electricity." Thus, the counterfactual claims at issue in the discussion must be construed in terms different from mere suppositions of reidentification.

zation as a "law" we undertake an epistemic commitment to retain it in the face of counterfactual hypotheses in such a manner that the conditional (A), viz., "If this wire were made of rubber then it would not conduct electricity" strikes us as natural vis-à-vis (B).[7] To treat a generalization as a law is to endow it with a status of inevitability—relative necessity—that gives it priority in cases of this sort.

That laws demand nomic necessity is one of the few points regarding which there is a substantial consensus in the history of philosophy. Aristotle insists on the matter in the *Posterior Analytics*.[8] It is a basic theme in Kant's *Critique of Pure Reason*.[9] And it continues operative in current writers. Such diverse authors as C. J. Ducasse, William Kneale, Ernest Nagel, and Arthur Pap, for example, hold that natural laws involve a necessity that is not logical but yet transcends merely *de facto* regularity.[10] Both Nelson Goodman and Roderick M. Chisholm have proposed hypothetical force as a prime criterion of the nomic necessity requisite for lawfulness.[11] And nowadays it is a matter of widespread agreement among philosophers that some characteristic mode of nomic necessity is involved in lawfulness, although there is much dispute as to just how the factor of nomic necessity is to be explicated. The writer of the pertinent article in the most recent philosophical encyclopedia puts the matter accurately by saying that the current point of dispute "is not

[7] The considerations at issue here are treated in more detail in my book on *Hypothetical Reasoning* (Amsterdam, 1965).

[8] See especially sections 1–6 of Book I.

[9] See especially the sections Introduction and Transcendental Analytic.

[10] See Curt J. Ducasse, "Explanation, Mechanism, and Teleology," *The Journal of Philosophy*, vol. 23 (1926), pp. 150–5; reprinted in H. Feigl and W. Sellars (ed's), *Readings in Philosophical Analysis* (New York, 1949). William Kneale, *Probability and Induction* (Oxford, 1939), p. 258. Ernest Nagel, *The Structure of Science* (New York, 1961). Arthur Pap, *An Introduction to the Philosophy of Science* (New York, 1962), see Chapter 16. Cf. also R. B. Braithwaite, *Scientific Explanation* (Cambridge, 1953), p. 293.

[11] R. M. Chisholm, "The Contrary-to-Fact Conditionals," *Mind*, vol. 55 (1946), pp. 289–307; reprinted in H. Feigl and W. Sellars (ed's), *Readings in Philosophical Analysis, op. cit.* Nelson Goodman, "The Problems of Counterfactual Conditionals," *The Journal of Philosophy*, vol. 44 (1947), pp. 113–28; reprinted in L. Linsky (ed.), *Semantics and the Philosophy of Language* (Urbana, Ill., 1952), and in N. Goodman, *Fact, Fiction and Forecast* (Cambridge, Mass., 1955).

about the propriety of using such terms as 'nomic necessity,' rather it is about the interpretation of these terms or the justification of their use."[12]

All the same, some recent writers have opted for a "regularity theory" of laws according to which lawfulness is to be construed as unrestricted factual generality pure and simple, so that no implicit claim of nomic necessity is called for. The *locus classicus* of opposition to nomic necessity is J. S. Mill, who emphatically rejected any interpretation of laws as necessitarian.[13] But in fact, his own position, analyzing lawfulness in terms of *unconditionality* as well as mere *invariableness*, in effect yields the core of what nomic necessitarians demand.[14] One contemporary writer has attempted a somewhat similar line, contending that the prime

objection to the regularity theory is that it cannot account for possible instances. If this charge were indeed well founded, it would be difficult to see how one could avoid the view that natural laws assert some kind of necessity such that they apply in all possible worlds. However, it is not established that a defender of the regularity view cannot give a plausible account of the application of laws to possible instances. He would argue that statements about possible instances stand in the same kind of logical relation to a law as do statements about actual unobserved instances. To the extent that a law enables prediction about unobserved instances, it enables justifiable claims about unrealized possibilities.[15]

Now it is easy to see that this line of defense will not serve at

[12] R. S. Walters, "Laws of Science and Lawlike Statements" in the *Encyclopedia of Philosophy*, P. Edwards (ed.), Vol. IV (New York, 1967), pp. 410–14 (see pp. 411–12). This article offers a very clear and compact survey of the key issues regarding laws.

[13] *A System of Logic*, Vol. II (London, 1834; 7th ed., 1868), pp. 419–21.

[14] For an interesting discussion of the historical issues see Gerd Buchdahl, "Inductionist versus Deductionist Approaches in the Philosophy of Science as Illustrated by Some Controversies Between Whewell and Mill," *The Monist*, vol. 55 (1971), pp. 343–67. For Mill see especially pp. 359–60.

[15] R. S. Walters, *op. cit.*, pp. 413–14. At least one influential adherent of the regularity theory was, however, prepared to brush aside all references to the possible, saying, "Physics wants to establish regularities; it does not look for what is possible." (L. Wittgenstein in his middle period as quoted by H. Speigelberg in the *American Philosophical Quarterly*, vol. 5 (1968), p. 256.)

all. It suffers from the critical defect of treating the unobserved and the unactualized cases in exactly the same way. But it is quite clear on even a little reflection that this step is indefensible because the unobserved and the unreal are in a totally different position in the context of inductive considerations, since the realm of the (heretofore) unobserved lies open to observational exploration, whereas the domain of the hypothetically unreal lies *ex hypothesi* beyond our reach. The unobserved and the unreal stand on an altogether different footing and must not be conflated with one another.

It is a crucial aspect of the lawfulness of laws that they serve not only for predictive purposes, but underwrite hypothetical and counterfactually assumptive reasonings as well. Their ability to support such suppositional reasonings is crucial, and yet if laws did not include the unactual in their scope, they could not support inferences of this type. If their sole observation-transcending concern were with the unobserved-but-real, the application of laws to the unobservable-because-unreal, could never be legitimated. A grasp upon the *unobservable* is something that laws could never obtain from a capacity to cope—however adequately—with what is merely *unobserved*.

Of course, one could try to argue that the consideration of hypothetical cases is improper or illicit (illegitimate, "beside the point," or whatever), that reality alone concerns us and that the unreal lies wholly outside the sphere of legitimate consideration. This does indeed abrogate the difficult nomic aspect of lawfulness. But it also writes off the prospect of hypothetical reasoning in the sciences and in consequence abolishes the concept of explanation as it has in fact developed in the setting of the Western tradition of scientific methodology.[16] The serious drawbacks of such a view are relatively obvious.

At this point the following line of reasoning stands before us: (1) to accept a straightforward regularity view of natural laws is simply to give up the prospect of distinguishing between accidental and lawful empirical generalizations, and so to jettison the

---

[16] This position is in fact taken by latter-day idealists of the type of F. H. Bradley and Brand Blanshard, who hold in effect that nomic necessity and logical necessity are indistinguishably one and the same, so that counterfactual hypotheses cannot be posed at all in any meaningful or coherent way.

conception of natural law that has been operative in Western philosophy from the days of Plato and Aristotle to those of Nelson Goodman, Roderick Chisholm, and Carl G. Hempel. And consequently, it is to abandon the concept of explanation operative in the West since antiquity, one that calls for the subsumption of the particular phenomena being explained under the covering generalizations of lawful purport. For if a law is *not* to be construed as having reality-transcending weight, then any prospect of its use in hypothetical reasoning is utterly destroyed. (2) But if the traditional conception of natural laws (as distinguished from simple regularities) is maintained, this requires us to recognize and acknowledge that central and definitive characteristic of laws: the fact that—through their essential support of counterfactual conditionals—they embrace applications to hypothetical as well as to actual cases, and that existent and nonexistent states of affairs alike fall into their sphere of application. And just this relevance to the sphere of unrealized possibility renders laws reality-transcending in a way that essentially introduces their nomically necessitarian aspect.

The conception of lawfulness maintained here places natural laws into a distinct and distinctive light. Laws claim more than mere regularity as such; for accidental universal truths also represent regularities, but cannot support counterfactuals in the manner quintessential to laws. But the laws at issue do not have the force and inviolability of *logical* truths: to gain the requisite necessity by *this* route is to pay too heavy a price. For we then could not (as in fact we can) reason coherently from contrary-to-law assumptions. ("If the law of gravitation were an inverse-cube relation, instead of an inverse-square one, then . . .") On the present view, lawfulness is a halfway house between mere regularity and logical principle: its nomic necessity is stronger than mere *de facto* truth but weaker than the logically apodeictic relations of abstract concepts. (Clearly, it is *natural* necessity that is at issue in a discussion of scientific laws: conceptual and logico-mathematical necessity does not fall within the purview of our analysis of transfactual claims regarding reality.) By their very nature, laws thus inhabit that area to which Hume would forbid all rational access: the domain between matters of fact on the one side and logical necessities on the other.

2. THE PROBLEM OF THE SOURCE OF NOMIC NECESSITY: THE INSUFFICIENCY OF EVIDENCE

The preceding discussion has argued at length that nomic necessity and hypothetical force are indispensable features of the laws used for the scientific explanation of events. This leads unavoidably to the question: Upon what evidential basis does an empirical generalization acquire the nomic necessity and hypothetical force it needs for lawfulness? It is clear upon reflection that however vast this evidential basis may be, and no matter how massively the substantiating data may be amassed through observation and experiment, and with whatever elaborateness the case may be developed, this evidential basis will always be grossly insufficient to the claim made when the generalization is classed as a law. This is so in part for the familiar reason that while all such evidence relates to the past and possibly the present, scientific laws invariably also underwrite claims about the future. Moreover, it is also made manifest when one considers the conceptual nature of lawfulness, bearing in mind that observation and evidence inevitably pertain to what happens *in fact*, whereas laws invariably also underwrite claims of a hypothetical or counterfactual kind.

Consider this matter of the insufficiency of the evidential basis for a law somewhat more closely. It is obvious that this basis will be *deductively insufficient*—insufficient, that is, when the argument is looked upon as being a deductive one—because the evidence inevitably relates to a limited group of cases while the applicability of the law is unrestricted. Moreover, the evidential basis will also be *inductively insufficient*. For the orthodox sorts of inductive procedures are designed to warrant the step from observed to unobserved cases, whereas a law—whose very lawfulness arrogates to it nomological necessity and counterfactual force—takes not only this inductive step from observed to *unobserved* cases, but also takes the added step from actual to *hypothetical* cases, and specifically to cases which, being fact-contradicting, are in principle unobservable. The inductive justification of hypothetical force would have to take the form "has always been applicable to counterfactual cases" to "will always be applicable to counterfactual cases." And the requisite premiss for such an induction must obviously always be unavailable.

The evidential foundation for lawful generalization is thus afflicted with a twofold insufficiency, not only in the *deductive* mode, but also *inductively*, at any rate as long as induction is construed along anything like usual and standard lines.[17] For induction as we know it is in principle impotent to yield any support for the counterfactual component inherent in laws. The crucial consideration is that the distinctive, transfactual content of a law is incapable *in principle* of receiving any *evidential* support along standard lines, because there can be no observational data regarding those instantiations (namely the counterfactual ones) that are distinctive of laws in contrast with the corresponding "merely accidental generalizations."

3.   LAWFULNESS AS IMPUTATION

The basic point, a point whose importance cannot be over-emphasized, is that the elements of nomic necessity and hypothetical force are not to be extracted from the evidence: they are not *discovered* on some basis of observed fact at all—they are *supplied*. It should almost go without saying that experience is of the actual alone: *the realm of hypothetical counterfact is inaccessible to observational or experimental exploration.*[18]

Lawfulness is thus not found in or extracted from the observational evidence, it is superadded to it.[19] *Lawfulness is the product of a transfactual imputation*: when an empirical generalization is designated as a law, this represents an epistomological status that is *imputed* to it. Lawfulness is something which a generalization could not *in principle* acquire on the basis of warrant by the empirical facts.

When one examines the explicit formulation of the overt *con-*

[17] For a cogent attack on the view that laws can be established by induction see K. R. Popper, *The Logic of Scientific Discovery* (London, 1959), Chap. III and New Appendix 10.

[18] It is obviously naïve to think that one can settle the question of the *counterfactual* application "If Caesar's chariot had been a satellite in orbit about the earth it would have moved according to Kepler's laws" by increasing the domain of *actual* applications of Kepler's laws in putting more spacecraft into orbit.

[19] On this point our whole analysis is at one with Hume's position. Cf. *A Treatise of Human Nature*, Bk. I, Pt. III, section 14. See §5 below for a discussion of the relationship of the present position and the relevant teachings of Hume and Kant.

tent of a law, all one can ever find is a certain *generalization.* Their syntactic structure as universal propositions of conditional type is all that law statements have in common as statements. Its lawfulness is not a part of what the law *asserts* at all—it is no part of its formulation and is nowhere to be seen in its overtly expressed content as a generalization. Lawfulness is not determined by what the generalization *says, but by how it is to be used in our reasoning.* By being prepared to put it to certain kinds of uses in modal and hypothetical contexts, *we, the users, accord to a generalization its lawful status,* thus *endowing* it with nomological necessity and hypothetical force. Lawfulness is accordingly not a matter of the assertive content of a generalization, but of its epistemic status as determined by the ways in which it is deployed for explanatory and predictive applications and in hypothetical reasoning.

Consider, for example, the law "Magnets attract iron filings" which supports the conditional "If this iron bar were magnetized (which it isn't), then it would attract these iron filings." As was argued in the preceding chapter, support of such counterfactuals is an indispensably essential feature of laws. Yet the establishment of such a relationship through the introduction of fact-contravening hypotheses rests in the final analysis on a point of epistomological policy: the determination so to use "genuine laws" (but *not* "accidental generalizations") as to give them priority in the resolution of a contradiction-forced choice created by the introduction of contrary-to-fact hypotheses (in the manner illustrated above). This, however, is not a matter of what the law *states* but of what is to be *done* with it: and so its lawfulness does not inhere in the meaning-content of the law-statement, but derives from "external" considerations, preeminently the precedence granted to it in counterfactual applications. Its being *lawful* is accordingly a feature of a generalization that is on much the same level with its being *axiomatic* or *important*: the issue is not one of the overt modes of formulation but of the uses to which it is put. (The axiomatic statement does not—and need not—*say* "I'm an axiom" and indeed the one that does say so need not *be* so.) Lawfulness is not a matter of semantic content, but of epistemic status.

This approach to lawfulness as imputed rests on a conception of the nature of scientific laws to which more explicit articulation must be given. Present-day philosophers of science have concentrated their attention primarily upon two aspects of "laws": (1) their *assertive characteristics*, having to do with the machinery deployed in their formulation (they must be universal generalizations, must be conditional in form, must make no explicit reference to time, must contain no overt spatial delimitation, they should be "simpler" than equally eligible alternatives, etc.), and (2) their *evidential status*, having to do with the nature of their supporting data (they must have no *known* counter-instances, they should be supported by an ample body of confirming evidence, etc.).[20] To considerations of these two kinds one must, however, add a third quite different factor. This relates to the issue of *epistemic commitment* and is the extent to which we are committed to retention of the law in the face of putative discordant considerations of a strictly hypothetical character (and thus not of an *evidential sort*, for this would lead back to item (2) above). The appropriateness of such epistemic commitment revolves about questions of the type: "To what extent is the 'law' at issue justifiably regarded as immune to rejection in the face of hypothetical considerations?" "How should this generalization fare if (*per improbabile*) a choice were forced upon us between it and other laws we also accept?" "How critical is it that the law be true—how serious a matter would it be were a law to prove false?"

This third factor represents an aspect of laws *crucially important to their status as laws.* For no matter what the structure of a generalization might be, or how well established it is by the known data, its qualification *as a law* demands some accommodation of it within the "system" of knowledge. Any "law" occupies a place that is more or less fundamental within the general architectonic of our knowledge about the world—its epistemic status is a matter not only of *its own* form and *its own* evidential support, but of *its relative placement within the complex fabric comprising it together with other cognate putative laws of nature.* The standing accorded to it within the overall framework of our knowledge reflects our "epistemic commitment" to the law, which is thus a matter not of the individual characteristics of the "law" viewed (insofar as possible) in isolation, but of its inter-

[20] See, for example, the excellent discussion in chap. 4 of Ernest Nagel's book on *The Structure of Science* (New York, 1961).

connections with and its epistemic rooting among other laws to which we are also committed. We must *decide* upon the epistemic status or ranking of the law with respect to others, and this decision, while in part guided by evidential factors, is not totally determined by them alone. It is a matter of a wide range of systematic considerations, among which evidential issues are only one (though to be sure a prominent) factor.

Lawfulness is accordingly a matter neither of *content* nor of *evidential basis,* but of systematic status in an epistemic setting. By examining an isolated generalization we can no more settle the issue of whether it is "really" a law than we can comparably settle the issue of whether an isolated mathematical thesis is "really" an axiom.

This axiomatic analogy holding that laws are essentially analogous to the axioms in a formalized system is crucial. It is notorious that there are many ways to axiomatize a given system and that the decision to endow a certain family of propositions with axiomatic status is based on various extra-systematic considerations (ease and elegance in proof construction, efficiency in establishing metatheorems, convenience in opening the system to an interpretation, etc.). Similar considerations obtain regarding the decision to grant certain generalizations the status of laws. These considerations are largely pragmatic in nature, and have to do with the way the generalization in question fits into the fabric of our picture of the world.

Clearly, on this approach, it is not the expressive *content* of a law that is decision-dependent—any more than the content of an axiom need be—rather, it is its *lawfulness* that is so dependent just as with the axiomaticity of the axiom.

4. WELL-FOUNDEDNESS

While laws are indeed man-made they are not thereby made *as man wants them.* In maintaining that the necessity and hypotheticality of lawfulness are matters of imputation, we thus have no wish to suggest that the issue is one of indifferent conventions or arbitrary decisions. The imputation is, to be sure, an overt step for which a decision is required. But to be *justified* this decision must be based upon a rational warrant, and must have its grounding in: (1) the *empirical evidence* for the generalization at issue in the law, and (2) the *theoretical context* of the generalization in terms of its systematic coherence within a broader framework embodying a fundamental view of the nature of the real world. Such evidential and systematic grounding is required to provide the necessary *warrant* to justify an imputation of lawfulness. Since an element of imputation is involved, laws are not just discovered, they are, strictly speaking, made. But this is not, of course, to say they are made arbitrary. Although they cannot be extracted from the empirical evidence, they must never contravene it. Such conformity with "the observed facts" is a key factor of that complex that bears the rubric of *well-foundedness*. To be sure, lawfulness can never be derived wholly from an observational foundation. But it represents an imputation that is (or should be) well-founded upon evidential grounds. The key factors in this well-foundedness are the *correspondence-to-fact* aspect of empirical evidence and the *systematic-coherence* aspect of fitting the generalization into a fabric of others that in the aggregate constitute a rational structure, an integrated body of knowledge that constitutes a "branch of science."

Our conception of the origin of the key requisites for a law (nomic necessity and fact-transcending hypotheticality) can thus be summarized in the slogan: *Lawfulness is the product of the well-founded imputation to empirical generalizations of nomic necessity and hypothetical force.* Both of these two factors, the essentially factual element of well-foundedness and the essentially decisional element of imputation, are necessary to laws. Well-founding is essential because the very spirit of the scientific enterprise demands reliance only upon *tested* generalizations that have a solid observational or experimental basis. But the element of imputation is also essential, since—as emphasized above—we can only observe what *is*, i.e., forms parts of the realm of the actual, and not what corresponds to the modally necessary or the hypothetically possible. The nomic necessity and hypothetical force characteristic of lawfulness thus represent factors that a generalization cannot conceivably earn for itself on the basis of observational or experimental evidence alone: it has to be *endowed* with these factors. The basic aspect of a lawful proposition is on this view not the *qualitative* aspect of being-a-law but the *relational* aspect of being-maintained-as-a-law. Lawfulness is in the final analysis a relational rather than an absolute and purely descriptive feature.

Yet, as we have seen, the conditions that establish a generalization as *law-like*—that is, as rationally *qualified* for an imputation of lawfulness on the basis of the usual methodological considerations—do not suffice to *establish* it as a law, i.e., as actually *lawful*. They fail in this because acceptance of a claim to lawfulness extends well beyond the factual basis upon which it is justified. To class a generalization as *law-like* is to say it is a *candidate-law* on the basis of factual considerations, but to class it as *lawful* is to step beyond this claim into the realm of nomic necessity and hypothetical force.

In saying that laws are man-made—that they are the products of a human decision to accord a certain status to specific generalizations—we do not intend to turn our back upon the work of methodologists of scientific inquiry and theorists of inductive logic. Insofar as their findings conform to the actualities of scientific practice there is no reason why we cannot—or should not want to—accept them in full. We are certainly not attempting a Quixotic substitution of "free decision" for scientific method. But we regard the principles of the theory of scientific method from our own perspective, and view them in what may well be a non-standard light. From our standpoint they are *not* procedures for the *establishment* of generalizations as lawful; rather, they are procedures for providing the rational warrant for imputation of lawfulness.[21]

---

[21] The first methodologist of science to take a position something like this was W. Whewell, who argued that (1) genuine laws must have the modal aspect of universality and necessity, (2) this can never be arrived at by reasoning from experience, and so requires a *sui generis* process (= our *imputation*), which "is not reasoning: it is another way of getting at truth," but (3) the offering of justified law-claims must have a proper empirical basis (= Whewell's "consilience of inductions"). The objections of modern critics to this procedure (see Larry Laudan, "William Whewell on the Consilience of Inductions," *The Monist*, vol. 55 [1971], pp. 368–91; see especially pp. 282–93) may be met by noting that Whewell does not offer the (self-contradictory) claim that the empirical basis establishes lawfulness in a *demonstrative* mode, but only that it warrants a rational claim to lawfulness in a *presumptive* mode. Whewell may not overtly have espoused the imputational theory of lawfulness, but once one does so, all of his characteristic doctrines on the subject fall smoothly into place.

The credentials of scientific method as procedures for providing this sort of rational warrant—both pragmatic (in terms of their practical fruitfulness) and Darwinian (in terms of the processes of historical selection on the basis of proven success)—are altogether impressive and in effect decisive. Just these considerations are crucial to the controls to which an imputational decision must be subject if it is to count as well-founded. And from our standpoint this pragmatic aspect of legitimation is crucial: the proof of the imputational pudding lies very much in the eating. It cannot be said too emphatically that the theory of lawfulness as imputation does not come to destroy the accepted procedures of scientific inquiry, but to fulfill the claims to law-validation generally made on their behalf. Our approach does not deny, but insists upon the crucial role of orthodox scientific method. (This assures the consonance of our present analysis of the nature of laws with that of the preceding chapter regarding the justification of "induction.")

5.   THE HERITAGE OF HUME AND KANT

This view of the nature of lawfulness carries Kant's Copernican Revolution one step further. Hume maintained that faithfulness to the realities of human experience requires us to admit that we cannot find nomic necessity in nature. Kant replied that such necessity does indeed not reside in observed nature, but rather in the mind of man, which projects lawfulness into nature in consequence of features indigenous to the workings of the human intellect.[22] Both Kant's and Hume's views share the

---

[22] A thread running through much of the history of philosophy is the thesis that there would be no laws if there were no lawgiver; that the universe would not be intelligible by man if it were not the product of a creative intelligence. We find this theme in Plato's *Timaeus*, in the cosmological argument of St. Thomas Aquinas and the schoolmen, in Descartes and Leibniz, in Butler's *Analogy* and the tradition of natural theology in England. Leibniz puts the matter cogently and succinctly:

   . . . the final analysis of the laws of nature leads us to the most sublime principles of order and perfection, which indicate that the universe is the effect of a universal intelligent power. (G. W. Leibniz, *Philosophical Papers and Letters*, ed. by L. E. Loemker, vol. II [Chicago, 1956], pp. 777–8.)

In this tradition, Kant's "Copernican Revolution" is decisive. Kant in effect agrees with the underlying thesis that the intelligibility and

characteristic aspect of our own position in having the consequence that laws, even natural laws, are in some measure *made*
by man rather than being altogether products of his *discovery*.

Our view of the matter agrees with Hume that lawfulness is
not an observable characteristic of nature, and it agrees with
Kant that it is a matter of man's projection. But we do not join
Hume in seeing this projection as a product of human psychology
and we do not join Kant in seeing it as the result of the (in suitable
circumstances) *inevitable* working of the cognitive faculty-
structure of the human mind. Rather, we regard it as a matter
of *warranted decision*, a deliberate man-made imputation effected
within the framework of a particular conceptual scheme regarding the nature of explanatory understanding. We thus arrive at a
position that is Kantian with a difference. Kant finds the source
of lawfulness in the way in which the mind inherently works. We
find its source in the conceptual schemata that men in fact deploy
in the rational structuring of human experience within the setting
of explanatory purposes. As we see it, lawfulness demands an
imputational step made in the context of a certain conceptual
framework of cognitive rationalization, and in particular of a
certain concept of explanation.

6. DOES THE SUCCESS OF SCIENCE INVALIDATE THIS POSITION?

The massive and striking success of the sciences in enabling one to
predict and control the course of natural events may seem at first
sight to militate against the acceptability of our position. If the
fabric of natural laws and the causal order of the universe are
seen as being in significant measure *the product of a mental
construction*, how are we to square this with their dramatic
success in prediction and control?

From our approach this *seeming* difficulty is not a real one. To
be sure, natural laws, according to our theory, possess a substantial
element of imputation and postulational construction. But as has
been stressed again and again, this is not a matter of *free* construction and *arbitrary* imputation. Our insistence on the element

---

rationality of the universe must be the work of an intelligent and
rational mind, but shifts the application of the principles from the
creator of the natural universe to the *observer* of it.

of well-foundedness and our adoption of the standard canons of scientific method for this purpose provide the means of mitigating the mentalistic factor of imputation. And in particular, the thesis that laws are linked to objective regularities in nature holds our feet to the ground in considering the "constructive" aspect of laws. (We have, to be sure, insisted that regularities *underdetermine* laws. A regularity—any perfectly genuine regularity—could be conceptualized as merely accidental, simply by not adding that "something more," the mind-involving factors of nomic necessity and hypothetical force indispensable for a claim of lawfulness.)

The idea—inherent in our position—that "the causal order of the world is a mental construct" may at the very first seem absurd and repellent. And deservedly so if there were no compensatory stress that this construction is not free or arbitrary, but must be well-founded and circumscribed by due heed of the established canons of scientific practice. Subject to such qualifications, however, it seems to me that the strangeness and unpalatability of the position evaporates. The success of science is no more inexplicable on our "idealistic" position than on any "realistic" rival. Indeed the case is very much one of parity on both sides. Where the one approach speaks of the "*discovery* of a law" (and immediately runs into the Humean difficulties of the justification of induction), the other speaks of "the warranting of an *imputation* of lawfulness" (and avoids these particular difficulties at one bold stroke). But given this difference of perspective all else is—with but minor readjustments—left pretty much the same. Both approaches demand the bridging of an evidential gap, a transition which the "realistic" theory sees as available in Hume-rebutting terms, and which the "idealistic" theory sees in conceptual scheme-justifying terms. The "realistic" approach collides with the fact that our evidence-in-hand can never come close to establishing the full spectrum of claims built into a law thesis. Our "idealistic" approach regards the standard conceptual scheme as so operative that no trans-factual justification is called for, since all that is needful is built into the workings of the imputation-laden concepts themselves. This leaves the problem that such an imputation-laden scheme might not be justified, but this turns out to be a very different and emphatically pragmatic story. An explanation of the success of science is called for on both sides of the divide, and turns out to be no more problematic on the idealistic than on the realistic approach. On the contrary, theoretical justification along the idealist/pragmatic lines is to all appearances more straight-forward and unproblematic. The essential facts of the structure of scientific inquiry and its results are altogether agreed upon; the crucial difference relates solely to the theoretical perspective from which these facts are to be viewed.

Indeed, the success of science is seen on our position as support-ing rather than countervailing consideration. The theory of law-fulness as imputation seeks its ultimate legitimation in the domain of practical reason. The propriety of imputation rests on the basis of an explanatory framework whose validation is ultimately forthcoming in practical terms of success in the prediction (= cognitive control) and manipulation (= operative control) of natural events. The warrant of the imputations one bases on the deployment of scientific method is thus supplied by the very success of science itself. From the angle of this Darwinian/prag-matic justificatory procedure, the success of science, rather than constituting an obstacle to our theory of lawfulness, provides the legitimation of the imputational step that is crucial to its work-ings.

7. IMPUTATIONISM

It is useful to supplement the preceding treatment of the im-putational theory of laws with some remarks about imputation or postulation as a methodological device of wider applicability. Indeed, the procedure of imputation is particularly important from the standpoint of the whole spectrum of "rationalist" points of view (owing to the attractiveness of the thesis that "the constitutive contribution of the mind to our knowledge of the world" is made by way of imputations).

This is particularly clear whenever a reality-characterizing claim goes beyond the confines of all possible experience and observation; that is, whenever a leap beyond the possibly avail-able evidence is made under the aegis of a conceptual scheme— exactly as we saw to be the case with respect to laws. The con-structive contribution of mind is particularly notable whenever one's claims regarding reality attribute to it features that could not

F

possibly be warranted as a matter of "observationally given fact."

The "problem of other minds" affords a paradigm example. All that one can ever "observe," in any relatively strict sense, in someone's behavior (e.g., his grimacing) but we conceptualize this mentalistically and so do not hesitate to say, quite properly, that we *see that* he is in pain (without in any way doing that impossible thing of seeing or sensing his pain). When we see his pain behavior we simply assimilate this case to our own situation "in similar circumstances" (e.g., when cut and bleeding). Knowing in first-hand experience that such occurrences are painful (to us) we project this by way of imputation to others. This imputational aspect marks the fact that the "seeing" of "seeing *that* he's in pain" is done not merely with the eye of the body, but with the mind's eye.

From this perspective, the crucial facts are these: (1) There is a decisive barrier between the manifestation of pain-behaviour on the one hand and the affective feeling of pain on the other—their fusion "in our own case" notwithstanding. (2) This barrier is not to be crossed by any valid sort of *inference* from behavioral premises to an affective conclusion. Rather, (3) it is leapt by an imputation that is built into a conceptual scheme determinative of the ground-rules governing our application of pain-talk.

This example and that of laws is, as we can see it, typical of that vast range of cases where the evidence-in-hand is in principle inadequate to the conclusion claimed. Thus, the leap from appearance ("*X* appears on the basis of observational inspection to have feature *F*") to reality ("*X* in fact has the feature *F*"), or again from teleological behavior of a sufficiently sophisticated kind to the possession of intelligence ("Can machines think?") are also essentially analogous to that of the leap from *post hoc* correlation to *propter hoc* causal connection that so troubled Hume and his latter-day congeners.

In all of these cases a decisive categorical barrier lies in the path of the direction of reasoning:

systematically observed instances $\rightarrow$ laws
pain behavior $\rightarrow$ feelings of pain
correlation $\rightarrow$ causation
appearance ("seems") $\rightarrow$ reality ("is")
teleological behavior $\rightarrow$ intelligent behavior

In such cases we cannot get from the left-hand item to the right-hand one by any sort of sound *inference* based on the observations in hand because we cannot secure the major premiss to warrant such an inference. In all cases we accomplish the rational transition at issue not by way of inference but by way of a mind-contributed imputation. But such an imputation is not a matter of human psychology (this is where Hume erred), but rather is built into the rational development of a conceptual scheme.

Thus, on such an approach, it is the logical placement of an imputation (postulation, rationally based assumption) within the framework of a conceptual scheme that is the crucial consideration. The imputation takes us beyond "the actual evidence in hand," but the entry of the conceptual scheme means that this is done in a rational, duly warranted, and objective or at any rate impersonal and interpersonal manner.

A cluster of imputations (or bases for imputation) is built into the very foundations of our conceptual scheme. Our *concepts* are designed to work in such a way that the seemingly unwarranted claim is rationally warranted because "that's what's being said": the conceptual scheme embodies a "theoretical" stance towards the world that embodies (and is the product of) certain imputations. Causes, material objects, persons are all theoretical entities built into a framework for organizing our thought about things. They are the conceptual *vehicles for imputation.* In a perhaps overly Kantian terminology, the application of such imputationally laden concepts might be characterized as conceptually immanent though empirically transcendent.

But the question remains: What justifies such imputation? In general, an imputation represents a constitutive thesis adopted on regulative grounds, as part of the venture of the theoretical rationalization of our experience. In the final analysis its status is methodological and its justification is accordingly to be given in the pragmatic terms of "working out"—of proving itself a successful instrument for the realization of the tasks in hand. And, of course, in the special case of imputation of lawfulness, the rational warrant is given in the first instance through an invocation of the canons of scientific method and in the final instance through more elaborately pragmatic considerations. But this line of justificatory argumentation involves large and far-reaching issues that lie outside the scope of our present theme (though I have dealt with them in another place).[23] The crucial fact is that the imputational approach is not dogmatic but, admitting the need for rational support, seeks to provide it mediately with reference to conceptual schemes and ultimately in pragmatic terms.

[23] For a more extensive treatment of the ideas of this section see the author's *Conceptual Idealism* (Oxford, 1973).

Chapter IV

THE PROBLEM OF NOUMENAL CAUSALITY IN THE PHILOSOPHY OF KANT

1. THE PARADOX OF NOUMENAL CAUSALITY

In the *Critique of Pure Reason*, Kant repeatedly characterized the thing itself (*Ding an sich* or noumenon) in such terms as "the nonsensible cause" of representations or as "the purely intelligible cause" of appearances (A 494=B 522). Again and again, he employs the language of causal efficacy in relation to things in themselves. Thus he speaks of "the representations through which they [things in themselves] affect us" (A 190=B 235) and elsewhere says of things in themselves that "they can never be known by us except as they affect us" (*Foundations of the Metaphysic of Morals*, Ak. 452) because the thing itself is a "transcendental object, which is the cause of appearance and therefore not itself appearance" (A 288=B 344). The thing in itself is described as "the true correlate of sensibility" which is not known, and cannot be known except through its representations (A 30=B 45).

But on the other hand, Kant is repeatedly and emphatically insistent upon the categorial fact that the linkage of cause and effect can only obtain as a relationship between phenomena, and that any applicability of the principle of causality is to be strictly confined to the phenomenal sphere. The categories and all that depends upon them just cannot apply to the thing in itself at all (*Prolegomena*, §§26, 28), and it must accordingly lie wholly outside the arena of causality. All possible knowledge of causal relations must lie within the empirical domain.

From the very outset, perceptive students of the Kantian philosophy such as J. S. Beck have been troubled by the question of how these two seemingly conflicting positions are to be reconciled.[1] And critics down to the present day continue to charge

---

[1] Kant himself was acutely aware of the problem. Already nine years before publication of the first *Critique*, he was wrestling (in the widely-discussed letter to Herz of 1772) with the issue of how a "representation that refers to an object without being in any way affected by it

Kant with outright inconsistency on this head. P. F. Strawson, for example, objects as follows in his book, *The Bounds of Sense* (London, 1966):

For the resultant transposition of the terminology of objects "affecting" the constitution of subjects takes that terminology altogether out of the range of its intelligible employment, viz., the spatio-temporal range . . . . the original model, the governing analogy, is perverted or transposed into a form in which it violates any acceptable requirement of intelligibility, including Kant's own principle of significance. (Pp. 41–2)

The issue of noumenal causality obviously poses a basic and important problem for any coherent interpretation of Kant's philosophy.

2.   SUFFICIENT REASON

I shall attempt to establish that, on the most plausible construction of Kant's view, two quite different sorts of "causality" are at issue here, viz. (1) *authentic causality* which is genuinely experientiable and is governed by the experientially *constitutive* Principle of Causality, and (2) a not properly causal *generic grounding* which is merely intelligible (i.e., can justifiably be *thought* but cannot be *known*) and is governed by a *regulative* Principle of Sufficient Reason. The kinship between the two sorts of "causality" is sufficiently remote that the employment of the same terms—such as "affecting"—in both cases must be regarded as merely analogical (in the manner in which Kant speaks at A 206 = B 251–2).[2]

---

can be possible"—a problem in which the anomaly of mixing non-causal representation with causal affection clearly arises. (The letter is translated in A. Zweig, *Kant: Philosophical Correspondence* [Chicago, 1967], pp. 70–6, and is discussed by L. W. Beck in "Kant's Letter to Marcus Herz, February 21, 1772," *The Philosophical Forum*, vol. 13 [1955], reprinted in *idem, Studies in the Philosophy of Kant* [New York, 1965].)

[2] Cf. also *Cr. Judg.*, §90. I find that the essentials of this view are anticipated, albeit with almost cryptic brevity, in A. C. Ewing's brilliant review of P. F. Strawson's *The Bounds of Sense* (in *Ratio* vol. 10 [1968], pp. 178–82). In particular I have in mind Ewing's insistence that "the

The key to a proper understanding of the role that Kant maintains for the thing in itself is his insistence that reason itself *compels* this:

For what necessarily forces us to transcend the limits of experience and of all appearances is the *unconditioned*, which reason, by necessity and by right, demands in things in themselves, as required to complete the series of conditions. (B xx; tr. Kemp Smith)

This passage not only says *that* reason demands the thing in itself, but also hints *why*. For Kant, the conception of a perceived object freed of the conditions of perception is every bit as senseless as would be that of a view-of-an-object that is freed from any and all *points of view*, and so regarded in separation from one of the essential conditions of viewability. But correlative with the conception of the conditioned object of perception goes that of an unconditioned noumenon. This conception is warranted and justified because it answers to the inexorable demands of a Principle of Sufficient Reason ("the unconditioned, which reason, by necessity and by right, demands . . . to complete the series of conditions").[3] As Kant puts the matter in one important passage:

The principle of [sufficient] reason is thus properly . . . a rule, prescribing a regress in the series of conditions of given appearances, and forbidding it [viz., reason] from bringing the regress to a close by treating anything at which it may arrive as absolutely unconditioned. (CPR, A 508 = B 536 — A 509 = B 537; tr. Kemp Smith)[4]

---

very concept of things-in-themselves must involve at least the category of causation since they can only be thought as the unknown ground of phenomena and ground is the category of cause as unschematized. . . . Strawson points out the inconsistency here, but he almost totally ignores Kant's attempt to remove it by his distinction between knowing and thinking according to the categories" (p. 182).

[3] Kant is not always careful to distinguish the generic Principle of Sufficient Reason from the specific Principle of Causality. For example, at A 201 = B 246 "principle of sufficient reason" is said where "principle of causality" is obviously wanted. Note however the explicit (and favorable) mention of the Principle of Sufficient Reason as an *a priori* synthetic principle in the *Prolegomena* (§ 3).

[4] The entire context of this passage is important. See also the key passage at A 305 = B 362 — A 307 = B 368.

There is a significant parallel between this passage and cognate discussions in Leibniz. Thus in explaining the workings of the Principles of Sufficient Reason in his important essay "On the Ultimate Origin of Things," Leibniz writes that:

. . . the sufficient reason of existence can not be found either in any particular thing or in the whole aggregate or series. . . . And even if you imagine the world eternal, nevertheless since you posit nothing but a succession of states . . . you find a sufficient for them in none of them whatsoever, and as any number of them whatever does not aid you in giving a reason for them, it is evident that the reason must be sought elsewhere. . . . From which it follows that even by supposing the eternity of the world, an ultimate extramundance reason of things . . . cannot be escaped.

The reasons of the world, therefore, lie hidden in something extramundane different from the chain of states or series of things, the aggregate of which constitutes the world.[5]

It is noteworthy—and characteristic of the writers involved—that whereas Leibniz here applies the Principle of Sufficient Reason *ontologically* to establish an extramundane source of our experienced existence (i.e., God), Kant applies it *epistemologically* to establish an extramundane source of our existing experience (i.e., the noumenon). Accordingly, the conception of a thing in itself represents for Kant the concept of an object whose nature is wholly unknown, in which all of the multiple representations of an experientially manifest object are mutually grounded, and thus rendered into appearances possessed of objectivity in being linked to *an object* (A 104, 109).

Of course, for Kant any such application of the Principle of Sufficient Reason would not succeed in bringing the *Ding an sich* within the orbit of experience. It remains something outside experience—and so unknowable—which, by the very workings of reason we not only can but must *think*, that is to say we must *postulate* it:

. . . all possible speculative knowledge of reason is limited to mere objects of *experience*. But our further contention must also be duly borne in mind, namely, that though we cannot *know* these objects

---

[5] "On the Ultimate Origin of Things" (1967) tr. by P. P. Wiener, *Leibniz: Selections* (New York, 1951), pp. 345–6.

as things in themselves, we must yet be authorized to *think* them as things in themselves; otherwise we should be landed in the absurd conclusion that there can be appearances without anything that appears. (B xxvi–xxvii)[6]

It is crucially important to recognize that Kant's step from appearances to the thing in itself is accomplished through the Principle of Sufficient Reason and *not* through the Principles of Causality. For causality, according to Kant, is operative only between phenomena, so that causal relations only obtain *within* the phenomenal realm. Any recourse to causality proper could never lead outside the area of the phenomenal: With the Principle of Causality, then, we must remain squarely inside the domain of experience.

But the operation of a Principle of Sufficient Reason can endow the phenomenal with an *intentional* character that points towards an external something outside the phenomenal domain. It does so by coming into play in a limited but very important way: by establishing the pivotal point that the phenomenal order must itself be grounded, and so producing the result *that* an underlying noumenal order must be accepted, without thereby going very far towards throwing light on the issue of *what* the nature of his noumenal order could be. Of course, such a circumstance cannot, on Kantian lines, be *known*—knowledge being confined to the realm of experience—but it can, and indeed *must* be *thought*.

In the *Prolegomena*, Kant articulates the line of thought at issue in the following terms:

Reason through all its concepts and laws of the understanding—which are sufficient to it for empirical use, that is, within the sensible world—finds in it no satisfaction, because ever-recurring questions

[6] This assertive use of to think = "think of as actually being the case" must be contrasted with the imaginatively speculative use of this same verb in such passages as "But I can *think* whatever I please, provided only that I do not contradict myself, that is, provided my concept is a possible thought" (Preface to the Second Edition). It is clear that in this latter passage *to think* does not mean "to think of as being *actually* so" but only "to think of as being *possibly* so." In Kant, as in ordinary speech, the verb is sometimes used in the one, sometimes in the other sense. Our concern here is throughout with its *assertive* as distinguished from its *speculative* use.

deprive us of all hope of their complete solution. . . . But it sees
clearly that the senuous world cannot contain this completion. . . .
The sensuous world is nothing but a chain of appearances . . . it is
not the thing in itself, and consequently must point to that which
contains the basis of this appearance, to beings which cannot be
known merely as appearances, but as things in themselves. In the
knowledge of them alone can reason hope to satisfy its desire for
completeness in proceeding from the conditioned to its conditions
(Ak. 353–4).

A careful heed of this perspective—and so of the distinction
between a generic (and regulative/methodological) Principle of
Sufficient Reason and a specific (and constitutive/substantive)
Principle of Causality—enables us to see how Kant can be freed
from the charge of inconsistency in regard to noumenal causality.
The answer is simply that *the relationship of the thing in itself
to the phenomenon is actually not to be construed in strictly
causal terms at all.* Kant's own occasional looseness of formulation notwithstanding, it is clear that while things in themselves
somehow "affect" the sensibility so as to bring representations
of objects into being, the relationship here at issue is definitely
not to be taken as causal. The linkage between phenomenon and
the thing in itself, rather than being actually causal in character,
is not mediated by the Principle of Causality at all, but by a more
basic and general Principle of Sufficient Reason. This principle is,
I submit, the (essentially) non-causal principle of grounding to
which Kant time and again makes appeal. And—use of activity-
oriented language notwithstanding—an appeal to actual causality
is just not at issue here: any more than when one says that 5 is
"produced" by the addition of 3 and 2. The relationships involved are essentially static linkages in a purely conceptual order.
Even with Kant we still sail in the backwash of the assimilation
inherent in the scholastic *causa* between a generic *grounding* of
reasons and a specifically efficient *causality* of natural process.[7]
The Principle of Sufficient Reason is, as it were, a pre- or sub-
categorical version of the Principle of Causality, even as an

[7] The word *Wirkung*, for example, is used in this generic way by Kant,
rather than being specifically limited to the cause-effect relationship. (Cf.
for example, the start of B 152 where Kant speaks of the transcendental
synthesis of imagination as "an action [*Wirkung*] of the understanding
on the sensibility.")

abstractly intelligible conception of grounding constitutes an unschematized counterpart to the conception of *cause*. In Kantian
jargon, *cause* is the specifically experiental schematization of the
essentially transcendental concept of a *ground*. The Principle of
Sufficient Reason is a *generic framework principle* guaranteeing
only *some* sort of grounding in general: the Principle of Causality
is a *specific implementation* of this principle indicating that in
one particular area (the domain of experience) one certain particular mode of grounding (viz., causal explanation) is always
forthcoming.[8]

If I am right in my view that a Principle of Sufficient Reason
is importantly at work in Kant's teaching, this opens up new
vistas in the comparative exploration in this regard between his
approach and that of Leibniz and Wolff. For the moment let it
suffice to state flatly that what Leibniz has in mind in elaborating
his Principle of Sufficient Reason is something very different.
Here, as elsewhere, the vicissitudes of philosophical history were
such that Kant was able to see the philosophy of Leibniz only
through a glass, darkly. Be this as it may, the key fact, I think,
remains that Kant's system of critical philosophy needs a Principle
of Sufficient Reason every bit as much as that of his "dogmatic"
predecessors, Leibniz and Wolff.

3. THE IMPETUS TO ONTOLOGICAL AUTONOMY AND INSUPERABLE
PROPENSITIES TO THINK

In order to see the systematic role of the Principle of Sufficient
Reason in Kant's thought in sharper perspective one must pay
closer heed to his conception of the objectivity of human experience. Any experienced object must—as it presents itself
within the orbit of sensory experience—inevitably fall subject
to the conditions of experientiability. In the framework of Kant's
philosophy, it makes no sense even to consider *this* object, the
experienced object, as somehow self-subsistent in the full bloom
of its mind-dependent qualifications as conforming to the precon-
ditions of experientiability. The object experienced is ineradicably

---

[8] Accordingly, Kant often speaks of the generic Principle of Sufficient
Reason when he intends the specific Principle of Causality, provided
that the context makes clear the relativization to the experiential
domain. See, for example, the start of A 201 = B 246.

heteronomous, it is inevitably qualified by the conditions of knowledge-conductive experience. But the mind leaps forward from the conditional object as given in experience to an un-shakable belief in a reality somehow hidden away under the superficial appearances we men take hold of.

The Kantian doctrine of the noumenal object roots in the final analysis in the structure of a certain conceptual scheme woven around the very concept of knowledge. For *knowledge* of objects would not be knowledge *of objects* if the "objects" at issue *did not have an ontological foothold outside the knowledge situation.*[9] But Kant in effect makes a subtle but crucial shift from the onto-logical to the epistemological order—from "did not in fact have" to "were not warrantedly thought to have." And what provides the validation for such a shift is a deployment of the Principle of Sufficient Reason.

We have here another aspect of Kant's Copernican Revolution. To have objective knowledge does not require us to know objects as things in themselves in order to control the correct-ness of our claims about them by way of a correspondence theory of truth. This is not required because it is in principle impos-sible. Rather, all that is necessary for "objectivity" is that certain logically essential conditions for the knowledge of objects be satisfied.[10] And the ultimate guarantee of the satisfiability of these logically essential conditions for objective knowledge is the

[9] In the second edition of the *Critique of Pure Reason*, where he is on his guard against being misunderstood as a radical idealist of the Berkeleyan stamp, Kant develops a cognate point in the following terms:

> Thus when I maintain that the quality of space and time, in con-formity with which, as a condition of their existence, I posit both bodies and my own soul, lies in my mode of intuition and not in those objects in themselves, I am not saying that bodies merely *seem* to be outside me, or that my soul only *seems* to be given in my self-consciousness.... It is only if we ascribe *objective reality* to these forms of representation, that it becomes impossible for us to prevent everything being thereby transformed into mere *illusion.* (B 69–70).

The point is that here too we must transform the objectivity at issue from the ontological order of what is so in actual, thought-independent fact, to the epistemological order of what is warrantedly thought to be so.

[10] This is why Kant's effective criterion of empirical truth is in the final analysis the standard of a coherence theory that proceeds by way of systematization. (See A 645 = B 673 to A 648 = B 676, and especially A 651 = B 680.)

Principle of Sufficient Reason, which—while it does not afford us knowledge regarding the realm of things in themselves—legitimates us in making claims about them by way of a warranted postulation.

Now if this leap toward the unconditioned behind conditioned objects as given in experience were not justified, then knowledge, objective knowledge, would collapse with it. Without the validation of our acceptance of an extra-experiential something that appears in experience, the claim to objectivity is cancelled: if it had no mind-independent basis, experience is stripped of any prospect of objective reference.[11] For then we could not legitimately regard the experience of objects as a *transaction*—the upshot of a genuine encounter between mind and object—but it would be a mere *production* of the mind alone. It is the fact that a justification *can* be given that shifts the Kantian position from a *subjective* to a *transcendental* idealism.[12]

[11] In the second edition of the *Critique of Pure Reason* Kant becomes even more emphatic on the realistic implications of this conception of objectivity:

> Thus perception of this permanent is possible only through a *thing* outside me and not through the *mere representation* of a thing outside me. (B 275.)

For Kant there is a significant distinction between *seeming* and *real* objectivity, a distinction whose legitimation requires us to postulate the realm of things in themselves, and one that is not only valid but crucial, since experimental *knowledge* could not possibly rest on a basis of merely *seeming* objectivity.

[12] A footnote is not the ideal place to ventilate a complex issue, but I would rather say here than not at all that while I take seriously the phenomenalist strain in Kant (i.e., his holding that the reality of physical objects lies in the fact that our experience has an appropriately systematic structure), I also take at face value his fundamental commitment to a realism of an altogether mind-independent *basis* for these mind-constituted things. The key to the reconciliation of these divergent strains seems to my mind to reside in the principle of individuation. For I take it that Kant's position is that experientially encountered particulars are inevitably individuated as such by the experiencing mind itself: specific individual particulars being mind-constituted—i.e., formed from the mind's imposition of a suitable ordering that operates with respect to a ground of generic and thinghood-lacking but altogether mind-independent basis. On this view, the realm of "*the thing* in itself" must remain a generic "night in which all cows are black"—rather than a structural plurality of differentiated "*things* in themselves" that correspond in a one-to-one fashion with the manifest particulars of our

It is crucially important for Kant that the ontological leap from appearance to underlying reality is justified. Yet for him this justification proceeds not in terms of ontology *per se*, but rather in terms of an ontology of mind. (The "Copernican Revolution" again.) The mind not only *can*, but it *must* assume or postulate an experientially untouched reality to underlie the experienced appearance by way of providing its grounding. Both the key terms here—"must" and "postulate"—require comment. But one central fact deserves restatement first: the mind engaged in the quest for knowledge approaches its experience with an insuperable impetus for ontological heteronomy, in virtue of which it insists upon (i.e., "necessarily postulates") the presence of an object that meets the demand for a reality to underlie appearance.

Back now to the formula that the mind *must postulate* a representatively efficacious and so, as it were, quasi-"causally" operative thing-in-itself as ground for the phenomenon. The "must" is critical here—because what goes on is no matter of idiosyncratic choice, but represents an essential feature of the human mind as such. In one key passage, Kant formulates the issue as follows:

[The] unconditioned is not, indeed, given as being in itself real . . .; it is, however, what alone can complete the series of conditions when we proceed to trace these conditions to their grounds. This is the course which our human reason, by its very nature, leads all of us, even the least reflective, to adopt. (A 583 = B 611 — A 584 = B 612; tr. Kemp Smith)

And again, in the *Prolegomena* Kant puts the matter in the following terms:

And we indeed, rightly considering objects of sense as mere appearances, confess thereby that they are based upon a thing in itself. . . . The understanding, therefore, by assuming appearances, grants the

ordinary experience. At any rate, these somewhat cursory indications may serve to indicate the lines along which I propose to construe Kant's insistence that physical objects, while empirically real, are transcendentally ideal, without (be it noted) construing this to mean that *everything* at the transcendental level is subject to ideality. For, from the transcendental angle, while the manifest particulars of our experience are indeed ideal, the thinghood-devoid (because thinghood-*underlying*) basis from which they result must be accepted as altogether real.

existence of things in themselves also; and to this extent we may say that the representation of such things as are the basis of appearances —consequently of mere beings of the understanding—is not only admissible but unavoidable (§ 32; tr. L. W. Beck)

This unavoidability is certainly important. There would be a very sorry defense of objectivity where one could not even get intersubjective universality. On first thought this unavoidability seems not to be a matter of *logical* compulsion. For logical compulsion is hypothetical while this the presently operative compulsion seems not hypothetical but categorical. Yet this appearance is misleading. We have here the sort of compulsion through rational presuppositions that is operative at many places in Kant. The necessitation at issue is thus not absolute but relative: *If you are going to claim* genuinely objective experiential knowledge, *then you must also be prepared to claim* a genuine object whose *existence* at any rate is something independent of the conditions of experience. That is, you "must" do this if experience is to be thought of in a certain way—i.e., is to count as *knowledge*-producing. In a key passage, Kant puts the matter as follows:

In the first place, it is evident beyond all possibility of doubt, that if the conditioned is given, a regress in the series of all its conditions is *set us as a task*. For it is involved in the very concept of the conditioned that something is referred to a condition, and if this condition is again itself conditioned, to a more remote condition, and so through all the members of the series. The above proposition is thus analytic, and has nothing to fear from a transcendental criticism. It is a logical postulate of reason, that through the understanding we follow up and extend as far as possible that connection of a concept with its conditions which directly results from the concept itself. (A 497 = B 526 — A 498 = B 526; tr. Kemp Smith)

So much, then, for the "must." Next we must consider "postulate"—for it is this, I submit, that Kant essentially means by "think" in the present context.

4. THE ROLE OF POSTULATION (ANNEHMEN)

The idea of postulation or supposition that is at work here has extremely important ramifications and implications, of which the following are crucial both in themselves and for Kant's purposes:

(1) When we "postulate" or "assume" something our very use of this indicates that we do not *know* this to be so. Postulation does not constitute knowledge, and its subject does not (*qua* postulate) represent something that we learn or discover or infer. (Of course, we can postulate something in one context and then learn later on in another context that it is so—but at that very point it stops being a postulate.)

(2) A postulate or assumption (as such) is not true or false, it is not correct or incorrect. It is precisely this fact that no claim of actual truth is involved at all, that underlies the previous point that postulation does not constitute knowledge.

(3) Though neither true nor false, a postulate or assumption can be warranted or unwarranted, useful or useless. Its status is instrumental or functional, and accordingly it can either be conducive to the purposes in view or fail to be so. It is in this, its functional role, that the validation of a postulate must be seen. Accordingly, the warrant of an assumption or postulate does not reside in its being true, but in *systematic considerations* regarding the cognitive context within which the postulate figures.

(4) In consequence, the role of a postulate or assumption is not *constitutive* but *regulative* (in Kantian terminology), that is, it does not represent an item of information that is part of our knowledge regarding how things go in the world, but is part of the instrumental or functional working machinery through whose operations we arrive at our knowledge.

I have gone into all this at some length partly because I think it useful in elucidating Kant, but also because I believe that the processes of postulation and assumption play an important role in the background of our knowledge, one that is regrettably neglected in current epistemology. If we restrict our epistemic vision too narrowly, we fall into the very trap against which Kant is trying to warn us—one into which his own critics not infrequently fall—the trap of holding that when something is in principle such that we cannot have *knowledge* of it, then it is also impossible that we should have rational warrant for thinking it to be so. Kant's crucial point is that not everything that we warrantedly think to be so will constitute knowledge. Quite the reverse, where *empirical* knowledge is concerned, there will have to be some precondition-pertaining thinkings-to-be-so that *must* be justified if a claim to knowledge is to be made good. Paradoxical though this may seem, the very possibility of objective empirical knowledge rests, for Kant, on a foundation of warranted postulation (i.e., on something that is not itself *known*).

From this point of view, Kant's agnosticism towards things in themselves must be taken very literally: to be sure, we can *know* nothing about them, but to say this is not to say that there is nothing that we can warrantedly assert regarding them (i.e., *think* about them—and not just imagine speculatively, but think "with assertive intent," to borrow Alonzo Church's form of words). Accordingly, there are various things we can *realize* about things in themselves (to introduce a technical term to contrast with *knowing*), viz., that they exist, that they are the [noncausal] ground of appearance, that they authenticate the objectivity of experience, that they are not spatiotemporal, that they behave lawfully [B 164], etc. Because we must be agnostic regarding things in themselves in the mode of empirical knowledge proper, we are still warranted in taking an emphatically realistic stance towards them—though this realm is, to be sure, not one of empirical knowledge but of transcendental postulation. Though essentially outside our capacity for knowledge (A 30=B 45), and representing, from the angle of our understanding an unsoluble problem (*Prolegomena*, 78), they are nevertheless the perfectly appropriate objects of a rational postulation; and so to deny us any *knowledge* of them is not to preclude all prospects of *information* about them.[13] The conception of a mode of informative

---

[13] Note that Kant does *not* hold with regard to things in themselves the difficult position that we can know they exist though we can know nothing whatever of their nature. Our information regarding their existence and their features rests on the same uniform basis, viz., rationally warranted postulation. The basic distinction between actual *knowledge* and postulation-based *information* is set out very clearly in the CPrR: "Therefore, through the practical law ... there is postulated the possibility of those [possible] objects of pure speculative reason, whose objective reality could not be assured by speculative reason [i.e., which it can *contemplate* but not *know*]. By this [postulation], then, the

cognition distinct from *knowledge* proper is central and crucial in Kant's philosophy.

Kant describes the noumenal postulation at issue in the validation of experiential knowledge in the following terms:

Appearances, so far as they are thought as objects according to the unity of the categories, are called *phaenomena*. But *if I postulate* things which are mere objects of understanding, and which, nevertheless, can be given as such to an intuition, although not to one that is sensible . . . such things would be entitled *noumena (intelligibilia)*. Now we must bear in mind that the concept of appearances, as limited by the Transcendental Aesthetic, already of itself establishes the objective reality of *noumena* and justifies the division of objects into *phaenomena* and *noumena*, and so of the world into a world of the senses and a world of the understanding (*mundus sensibilis et intelligibilis*). . . . For if the senses represent to us something merely *as it appears*, this something must also in itself be a thing, and an object of a non-sensible intuition, that is, of the understanding. . . .

All our representations are, it is true, referred by the understand-

theoretical knowledge of pure reason does not obtain an accession [of further knowledge], but it [i.e., the postulation] consists only in this— that those concepts which for it are otherwise problematical (merely thinkable) are now described assertorically as having objects, because practical reason inexorably requires the existence of these objects...." (Ak., p. 134; tr. L. W. Beck with my bracketed interpolations.) The process of postulation comes into central prominence in the second Critique, where it is deployed in a strictly *practical* role, but, as our discussion shows, it is already present in the first Critique in its essentially *regulative* role. And whatever the difference in function, it is essentially the same process that is at issue in the two cases.

In the *Critique of Judgment*, Kant returns to the matter in the following terms: "To prevent a misunderstanding which may easily arise, it is in the highest degree needful to remark that, in the first place, we can *think* these properties of the highest Being only according to analogy . . . in this way we only *think* the supreme Being; we cannot thereby *cognize* Him and ascribe anything theoretically to Him. It would be needful for the determinant judgment in the speculative aspect of our reason to consider what the supreme world cause is in Himself. But here we are only concerned with the question, what concept we can form of Him, according to the constitution of our cognitive faculties, and whether we have to assume His existence in order merely to furnish practical reality to a purpose, which pure reason without any such presupposition enjoins upon us *a priori* to bring about with all our powers. . . ." (§88 *ad fin*; tr. J. H. Bernard; cf. also §91 *ad fin*.)

ing to some object; and since appearances are nothing but representations, the understanding refers them to a *something*, as the
object of sensible intuition. But this something, thus conceived, is only
the transcendental object; and by that is meant a something $= X$,
of which we know, and with the present constitution of our understanding can know, nothing whatsoever. (A 249–250; tr. Kemp
Smith; my italics)

The rationale of this postulation is described from a somewhat
different perspective in the *Critique of Practical Reason*:

Even the concept of causality, having its application and hence
significance only in relation to appearances which it connects into
experiences (as shown in the *Critique of Pure Reason*), is not enlarged
by this reality [of the moral law] so as to extend its employment
beyond these limits. For if reason sought to go beyond them, it
would have to show how the logical relation of ground and consequence could be synthetically used with another kind of intuition
than the sensuous, i.e., how a *causa noumenon* is possible. This
[theoretical or speculative] reason cannot do, but as practical reason
it does not concern itself with this demand [for a theoretical demon-
stration], since it only posits [i.e., postulates] the determining ground
of the causality . . . ; it does so not in order to know objects but only
to define causality in respect to objects in general. (Ak., p. 49; tr.
L. W. Beck)

Again, in the *Critique of Judgment*, Kant returns to this issue
of postulation in the context of validating the conception of the
purposiveness of nature as a practical postulate. The postulation
operative there is also illuminating for present purposes:

It is only objects of pure reason which can be things of faith at all,
though not as objects of mere pure speculative reason. . . . They are
ideas, i.e., concepts whose objective reality of which we cannot
ascertain theoretically. On the other hand, the highest final purpose
to be attained by us . . . is an idea which has, in a practical reference,
objective reality for us and is something [real]. But because we cannot furnish such reality to this concept from a theoretical approach,
it is a mere thing of faith of the pure reason, along with God and
immortality, as the conditions under which alone we, *in accordance
with the constitution of our (human) reason*, can conceive the possibility of the efficacy of the use of our freedom in conformity with
law. But belief in things of faith is a belief of purely practical aspect,

i.e., a moral faith, which proves nothing for theoretical pure rational knowledge. .... If the supreme principle of all moral laws is a postulate (*ein Postulat*) so is also the possibility of its highest object, and consequently, too, the condition under which we can think this possibility is postulated along with it and by it. Thus the cognition of the latter—regarded as theoretical cognition—is neither knowledge nor opinion of the being and character of these conditions, but is a mere assumption of a practical import that is commanded for the moral use of our reason. (§91)

Patently, when we *postulate* a thing, use of the very word "postulate" (or "assume" or "suppose") concedes that (1) we certainly do not encounter this thing in *experience*, and in fact (2) we do not actually *know* that it exists. But, of course, postulation is a step not to be taken at haphazard: it must have some rational foundation for its justification, some sort of *validation*. And this in the present instance lies in its systematic role as part of the rational foundations of knowledge. And it is at just this point that the Principle of Sufficient Reason enters in. The operation of the Principle of Sufficient Reason in its regulative guise can provide the needed warrant for this necessary postulation of an extra-experiential something that underlies experience.[14] The Principle of Sufficient Reason is able to play this justificatory role not because of its status as an *a priori* truth (for then its validity would have to be intra-experiential) but because it repre-

---

[14] "The principle of [sufficient] reason is thus properly only a *rule*, prescribing a regress in the series of the conditions of given appearances, and forbidding it [i.e., reason] to bring the regress to a close by treating anything at which it may arrive as absolutely unconditioned. . . . Nor is it a *constitutive* principle of reason, enabling us to extend our concept of the sensible world beyond all possible experience. It is rather a principle of the greatest possible continuation and extension of experience, allowing no empirical [i.e., intra-experiential] limit to hold as absolute. Thus it is a principle of reason which serves as a *rule*, postulating what we ought to do in the regress, but *not anticipating* what is present *in the object as it is in itself, prior to all regress.* Accordingly I entitle it a *regulative* principle of reason. . . ." (A 509 = B 537). The violation of this restriction lies at the base of the antinomies: "The whole antinomy of pure reason rests upon the dialectical argument: If the conditioned is given, the entire series of all its conditions is likewise given; objects of the senses are given as conditioned; therefore, etc." (A 497 = B 525).

sents a regulative principle whose operation forms part of the possibility-conditions of objective experience.[15]

The idea of existential postulation may seem strange, and perhaps the whole process may be thought illegitimate. I should like to give an example that may remove some of this aspect of strangeness. Consider the question of the *sum* of an infinite series such as

$$\tfrac{1}{2} + \tfrac{1}{4} + \tfrac{1}{8} + \ldots + \tfrac{1}{2^n} + \ldots$$

Clearly, we can never sum the series up to show that the sum-total in question exists: we not only cannot produce the infinite sum, we cannot even demonstrate (and so *know*) its existence by machinery of arithmetic. (All that we can demonstrate is the conditional fact that *if* the sum exists, then it can neither be greater nor less than 1—we cannot demonstrate categorically that it exists and equals 1.) But we postulate the existence of infinite sums—whose existence we admittedly cannot *prove* in the usual way—then we are in a position to make claims regarding the sum-total of our series. This example, then, may serve to motivate by way of analogy the conception of an existential postulation.

The example has close kinship to Kant's line of thought. We can demonstrate that the sum

$$\tfrac{1}{2} + \tfrac{1}{4} + \ldots$$

is subject to a limit—in that it cannot possibly exceed 1. But the actuality of a limit to a series i.e., of a series being limited, does not establish the existence of something *at* the limit, something that does the limiting—as Kant clearly says in the *Prolegomena* §45 (Ak. 332). Similarly, the limitedness of a regressus of grounds does not establish the existence of an ultimate ground, knowable in the same manner as the grounds themselves. To say that such a limit can—and in certain cases *must*—be *thought* to exist, is to say that its existence can be *known*. A *limit of known grounds* does not constitute a *known limit of grounds*.

This illustration of an unattainable and purely implicit limit is formative in the background of Kant's line of thought. Behind the phenomenally given and conditioned—never overt and ex-

---

[15] The conception of an existential postulation again plays a central part in the argument for the existence of God in the *Critique of Practical Reason* (see Bk II, ch. ii, sect. 5).

plicit but ever-present in a hidden and implicit way—lies the work of the conditioning factors that give them shape and structure, the organizational "vanishing point" (*focus imaginarius*) of our cognitive perspective. This comparison serves Kant to illustrate the modes of conditioning which our knowledge inevitably *displays* but never overtly reveals, and towards which our cognizing irresistibly points but yet never actually reaches.

5. CONCLUSION

The crux of our position, then, is that *noumenal* "causality" is not actual causality at all, in the strict sense in which causality is governed by a specific, experientially constitutive Principle of Causality. Rather, it is only analogical causality, governed by a generic and regulative principle of grounding, a Principle of Sufficient Reason. And this is a principle that controls what we must *think* to be the case, rather than what we can claim to *know* regarding nature; it validates a postulation rather than establishes a fact. Hence, this use of Principle of Sufficient Reason does not demonstrate the *existence* of noumenal grounding. What it does is to afford a rational basis for the warranted (indeed, as Kant has it, *necessary*) postulation of noumenal causality in terms of Kant's know vs. think distinction. The Principle of Sufficient Reason accordingly provides the basis of postulation that is both inevitable and rationally warranted.

This principle thus does a job that needs doing for Kant and that other items of his system are not prepared to do. The Principle of Sufficient Reason is for him regulative: it signalizes a divine discontent, the unwillingness—nay inability—of the human mind seeking objective knowledge to rest satisfied with conditions and to abstain from an insistence upon the unconditioned. But it also marks the critical limit that sets knowledge off from thinking (sc. postulating). The fact that a principle with a systematically solid standing is involved is crucial here, for only through such a systematic principle could we obtain a rational *warrant* for the postulation that calls noumenal causality into operation.

Kant made a strikingly daring innovation in holding that man's objective knowledge of the world about us rests, in the final analysis, on the employment of validating principles that are postulated rather than discovered, and are knowledge-productive rather than knowledge-produced. These principles do not have the shaky status of "mere assumptions" or "arbitrary stipulations," but are *warranted* postulations whose legitimation rests on ultimately *regulative* conditions. This stress on the controlling role for our knowledge of regulative principles whose validation lies ultimately with the active aspect of man as knowledge-producer, rather than the passive aspect of man as knowledge-possessor, represents a basic Kantian insight of enduring value. Its interest survives any cavils, however justified, regarding this or that detail of his magesterial system.[16]

POSTSCRIPT

The position of the present book is crucially indebted to the Kantian doctrine elucidated in this chapter: the thesis that the *consitutive* view regarding matters of fact taken in our systematization of empirical knowledge in science and common life is crucially dependent upon certain postulations or imputations whose status is strictly *regulative* in nature. However, we move beyond this Kantian position in insisting that the validation of the regulative principles at issue is itself ultimately practical or pragmatic (rather than seeing it to lie, à la Kant, in the very faculty structure of the human intellect). For Kant himself the justificatory role of practical reason relates to issues more transcendental than that of the rational foundations of empirical knowledge. On our approach, however, the lines of thought of the second Critique are projected back into the considerations of the first. In maintaining that even the regulative principles of our factually constitutive, scientific knowledge of empirical fact call for the legitimizing services of practical reason, our Kantian position becomes *plus royaliste que le roi.*

[16] This chapter is a much-expanded version of the author's paper on "Noumenal Causality," *Proceedings of the Third International Kant Congress* (Dordrecht, 1972), pp. 462–70.

Chapter V

ON THE SELF-CONSISTENCY OF NATURE

I. BACKGROUND

That this world of ours is self-consistent, that the domain of reality is free from all inconsistency and self-contradiction, is among the prime tenets of the mainstream of philosophical tradition stretching from the Presocratics to the present day. This thesis that absence of contradiction is a key test of objective reality can be found in Parmenides and Plato, in various sectors of the skeptical tradition, in rationalists like Leibniz, in empiricists like Locke, in idealists like Bradley, and among the great bulk of our own contemporares of all persuasions.

There is one seeming exception to the contention that this position is the rule among philosophers. Hegel certainly regarded inconsistency as a central factor in philosophy, and the conflict of opposites is a key aspect of that ebb and flow of thesis and antithesis, of impetus in opposed directions that constitutes the fabric of the Hegelian dialectic. But such a conflict and ambivalence in the thoughts and actions of individuals—can readily be conceded without maintaining that reality is in fact inconsistent in the hard sense of actual self-contradiction as the logicians have taught us to understand it. Thus, for example, while Marxists are constantly expatiating upon the "contradictions" of capitalism, it is clear that they in effect mean no more than that capitalist societies exhibit deep internal conflicts, mutually destructive tendencies, and inner antagonisms. Such Hegelian so-called "contradictions" have to do with inconsistencies and instabilities, with inner tensions and strains and opposite pulls. There is nothing actually *inconsistent* about any of this in the logically rigoristic sense. Outright self-contradiction as the logicians explicate it—as transgressions of the Law of Contradiction—is not at issue.

As logicians since Aristotle have viewed the matter, to have an instance of inconsistency or self-contradiction we must confront a situation where *something both is and is not so.* Thus consider a case where in some circumstances X (a society say, or an individual) will do A and not B, and in other cases, precisely similar in character, X will do B and not A. There is, of course, nothing logically self-contradictory about this. It is not *contradiction* that we face here, but a lack of uniformity, a failure of that consistency of thought and practice which calls for treating like cases alike. Now, of course, we would ordinarily not hesitate to say that someone who behaves in this reckless and unstable way is being *contradictory* in his actions, and to say that what he did in one case was *inconsistent* with what he did in the other. But our ordinary use of the term in common speech is somewhat undemanding: what it points towards is not a logical contradiction but simply a failure to realize the Kantian ideal of universality—of having what we do or say conform to a fixed general rule of principle. And *this* sort of inconsistency, to wit lack of *uniformity*—a failure to talk or act in a constant and stable way as between various occasions—is again hardly an instance of logical inconsistency in the Aristotelian mode. There is, after all, nothing *logically* peculiar (let alone impossible) about a lapse in uniformity, a failure to maintain strict regularity. Any genuinely stochastic process in physics—the radioactive decay of atoms of a very heavy element, for example—will conform to exactly this pattern that:

In some cases X will do A and not B [say an atom with half-life of 1 year will decay within 6 months and not last over a year], whereas in other *precisely similar* cases X will do B and not A.

The disuniformity of a failure to follow a fixed deterministic rule, is presumably commonplace in nature: there is nothing contradictory or self-incompatible here.

The hard-core of the question of the constituency of reality does not relate to the issue of Hegelian harmony (freedom from internal conflicts) or Kantian universality (realization of internal uniformity). The key issue is that of Aristotelian inconsistency, the self-contradictoriness of the logicians.

But now with *this* sense in view, might not something both be the case with respect to nature and not be the case? Could something—somehow—be and not be so?

This question must be considered with at least as much clarity and precision as Aristotle managed to give it over two millenia ago. It is well worth giving heed to his formulation of the issue in the tract *On Interpretation* (*De interpretatione*):

Thus it is clear that for every affirmation there is an opposite negation, and for every negation an opposite affirmation. Let us call an affirmation and a negation which are opposite a *contradiction*. I speak of statements as opposite *when they affirm and deny the same thing of the same thing—unequivocally*; together with all other such conditions that we add to counter the troublesome objections of sophists. . . . Of contradictory statements about a universal taken universally *it is necessary for one or the other to be true or false*; similarly if they are about particulars, e.g., "Socrates is white" and "Socrates is not white." (*De interpretatione*, chap. 6, 17a28–17b29)

Clearly, two key points of these remarks are (1) that contradictory affirmations and negations must be construed unequivocally *as obtaining in precisely the same respect*, and (2) when so construed, then they cannot both be true.

The focal idea and leading principle of this explanation of the "Law of Contradiction" (or better *Noncontradiction*) as it is generally called is that something cannot both be and not be so unequivocally and *in one and the selfsame respect*. Of course, a substance can be hard by one standard of comparison and not hard by another, but if the situation is considered subject to a definite and unequivocal specification of the respect at issue, then only one outcome as regards a characterization as hard or not hard is possible. Given the key factor of a uniformity of respect, Aristotle maintains that the Law of Noncontradiction takes hold. And virtually the whole of the Western tradition in the philosophy of logic stands with him on this point.

2.   WHAT WOULD AN INCONSISTENT WORLD BE LIKE?

What, after all, would an inconsistent world be like—one that violates the requisites of self-consistency in the strong (logical, Aristotelian) sense? Such a world would have to have the feature that in some perfectly definite way something both is and is not so. Definite, that is, in that *all* relevant respects would have to be identical. None of your subterfuges about something being both malleable and not malleable because it is malleable in one circumstance and not in another. Or consider a somewhat more realistic example. Take the two theses:

(W) Light emissions behave in the manner of waves and not particles.

(P) Light emissions behave in the manner of particles and not waves.

A certain sloppiness prevails here, for one would need first to specify in some detail what sort of wave-ly or particle-y behavior was at issue. But supposing this appropriately done, the theses (W) and (P) will certainly conflict with one another: they could not possibly both be said of one selfsame world without logical incoherence: each as it were takes away what is given by the other. As they stand, (W) and (P) are simply not *co-tenable*. Their juxtaposition could, of course, be saved by some slight modification to restore mutual harmony. For example, we might contemplate the modification

(W') In circumstances of Type I, light emissions behave particly, not wavily.

(P') In circumstances of Type II, light emissions behave wavily, not particly.

Now as long as no circumstances whatsoever conform to the conditions *both* of Type I and Type II, all is well. There is no conflict of contradiction between the reformulated versions. But should some case (be it actual or possible) exhibit *both* of these Types I and II, then hopeless difficulties would come upon us. For then the crucial element of sameness of respect from which a contradiction obtains its real bite would be present.

But now let us assume that worst has come to worst and that we are confronted with the situation of an actual outright logical conflict in the characterization of the real. Suppose, in short, that reality were inconsistent: let it be supposed that all the relevant issues about sameness of respect have been settled, and now something both is and is not so. What then?

Clearly, only one rationally viable upshot is now possible. We have no choice but to regard *the very hypothesis we are making* as self-destructive, as simply annihilating itself. That is, the demands of intelligibility constrain us to the position that it is not *nature* that is self-contradictory (and ultimately unintelligible) but the very assumption that we are being asked to make about it.

On this point the correct view is surely that of the essential Kantian insight: we must hold that consistency (or rational intelligibility) is not a *constitutive* feature of nature—not, that is, ultimately a properly descriptive characteristic of it—but a *regulative* feature; an aspect, that is, of our *concept* of nature, of the way in which we thinking beings do *and must* conceptualize it if the interests of minimal intelligibility (viz., logical viability) are to be achieved. On such a view, consistency is not a constitutive and empirical (i.e., experientially discovered) descriptive feature of the world, but is, in the final analysis, a regulative and conceptual feature of our understanding of it, an aspect—to be blunt—not of *reality* as such but of our procedures for its conceptualization and accordingly simply of *our conception* of it.

From this standpoint it becomes clear that the contention that nature is self-consistent is in the final analysis not really descriptive of *nature* at all, but inheres in the language-embedded conceptual machinery that we deploy for talking and thinking about it. The consistency-of-nature thesis becomes, in effect, a regulative principle for conceptualization. Its foundation is epistemologico-conceptual and not ontological, and the ultimate source of the putative noncontradictoriness of nature lies in "the mind," rather than in the mechanisms for the conceptualized "reality" itself. Consistency, in short, is seen as ultimately inherent in the mechanisms for the conceptualized constituting of *our* world rather than as somehow representing a facet of the world *an sich*.

3. THE BORGES WORLD

Now if this "merely conceptualistic" view of the self-consistency of the world is accepted, does it not then come to be a genuine possibility that reality itself might verge upon being inconsistent?

One attractive way of getting round this problem is to dissipate it by a bit of philosophical analysis. We would begin by noting that there is no point (and no content) in the concept of "reality itself" as wholly apart from *some possible conceptualization* of it. But if this is so, then surely if all of its possibly tenable conceptualizations are self-consistent, then it is pointless and vacuous to consider the prospect of "reality itself" as variant in this regard.

But this way of looking at the matter, while presumably correct, and undoubtedly in the approved philosophical mode, also has a certain quibbling air about it. From a more unsophisticated standpoint, the answer to the question is that reality might indeed come very close to self-inconsistency, so close as virtually to get there.

The best way I can think of to elucidate this prospect is by reference to one of the stories of that brilliant Argentenian writer of metaphysical science fiction, Jorge Louis Borges. In his short story, "The Garden of Forking Paths,"[1] published in 1941, Borges envisages a fictional work (by an equally fictional author, Ts'ui Pen) that is the complex history of a world in which *all alternative possibilities are concurrently realized*:

In all fictional works, each time a man is confronted with several alternatives, he chooses one and eliminates the others; in the fiction of Ts'ui Pen, he chooses— simultaneously—all of them. . . . Here, then, is the explanation of the novel's contradictions. Fang, let us say, has a secret; a stranger calls at his door; Fang resolves to kill him. Naturally, there are several possible outcomes: Fang can kill the intruder, the intruder can kill Fang, they both can escape, they both can die, and so forth. In the work of Ts'ui Pen, all possible outcomes occur; each one is the point of departure for other forkings.[2]

This train of ideas leads to the following daring conception:

A *Borges world* (as I shall call it) is one in which *all* of the distinct alternatively possible outcomes of a contingent situation are *jointly* realized. It is one internally complex world embracing distinct and discordant actualities. It is a world in which if one *can* spend an evening in each of several ways, one proceeds to spend it in all of them: a world in which when I can either eat my cake or have it, I simply do both; a world where in fact "you *can* have it both ways." The "reality" of such a world is intrinsically manifold and alternative-embracing, because all genuinely possible alternatives are actualized. It is a world in which the distinction between possibility and actuality collapses—not because there is never more than one possible alternative but because *all* of the alternative, seemingly mutually excluding possibilities are

---

[1] First published in 1941 in his narrative collection *El jardin de los senderos que se bifurcan* (Buenos Aires, Sur, 1941). I quote from J. L. Borges, *Labyrinths: Selected Stories and Other Writings* by ed. D. A. Yates and J. E. Irby (Penguin Books: Harmondsworth, 1964).

[2] J. L. Borges, *op. cit.*, p. 51.

conjointly actual.[3] And this leads to the concept of what I shall call the *Borges hypothesis*: the theory that this, our own actual world, is a Borges world.

4.   THE EVERETT-WHEELER THEORY

One's natural reaction to such a prospect might be a determined refusal to take it seriously, viewing it as the bizarre and aberrant product of literary speculation of the science-fiction category. This would be a grave mistake.

In recent physical theory the Borges hypothesis has received the accolade of scientific advocacy. It has come into its own in being advanced as a serious scientific theory, moving the roadways of the physical literature under the name of the Everett-Wheeler theory in quantum mechanics.

Let me describe briefly the formulation of this theory.

The focal point is the issue of measurement in quantum theory, specifically the well-known "problem of the reduction of the wave pocket." With such quantum theory measurement cases as the nucleonic decay-timespan of a very heavy radio-active element, the result of a measurement is formally speaking a superposition of vectors, each representing the quantity being measured as having one of its possible values; that is, each being a distinct, observational result of measurement. The obvious difficulty is how this superposition of distinct outcomes can be reconciled with the fact that in practice only one value is to be observed. How is it that in experimental trials at quantum measurement only one unique single outcome can be encountered observationally when the theory itself provides no means for collapsing the state vector into a single one of its values? How can the process of actual observational measurement force an inherently pluralistic situation into producing a unique result?

The orthodox quantum-theoretical line of response to this question is to say that only one outcome is real, and that the other alternatives are *unactualized possibilities*, merely possible but utterly nonactual alternatives. The fundamental problem of this approach is put by the question: How can an experimental

---

[3] It is, of course, *physical* possibility that is at issue at this stage of the discussion, and not logical possibility.

trial of physical measurement single out as uniquely real and actual one specific situation whose status in all departments of physical theory altogether similar to that of others. Given that physics is inherently nondiscriminatory as between these alternatives, how is the measuring process able to contrain nature to select one single alternative as the uniquely real observed value? How can a measurement force reality to make up its mind, so to speak?

The Everett-Wheeler hypothesis cuts the Gordian knot of this problem by the daring thesis that *all* of the possible alternative outcomes are in fact actual. We come here to its notorious hypothesis of the "self-multiplication of the universe." Intuitively, its physical picture is that of a universe continually splitting into a multiplicity of distinct but equally real subworlds, each embodying a unique but definite result of the quantum measurement. The cosmos is the internally complex counterpart of a linear superposition of vectors, each of which represents observable reality as having assumed one of its value outcomes. The seeming uniqueness of the quantum observation is a simply *perspectival* aspect of the relationship between the observer and what is observed: being placed within the subworld where a given result obtains, the other no less real outcomes are simply observationally inaccessible to the observer. The reason why all observers agree on a given result inheres in the merely parochial fact that they hail from the same subworld, and accordingly lack all prospect of causal interaction with the rest. We have simply lost to another subworld those observers whose view of reality conflicts with our own.

It is worth noting that this doctrine carries to its logical conclusion the tendency of the Copernican revolution to move away from the anthropocentrism of the Aristotelian world-picture. We standardly draw the familiar distinction between this, the actual world and other physically possible but unrealized worlds. From the standpoint of the Everett-Wheeler hypothesis it is unduly anthropocentric to view this world of ours as the uniquely actual one: We are bid to recognize the other physically realizable worlds as wholly on a par with ours in point of actuality. That they are inaccessible to us is—as it were—our misfortune, and not theirs.

The development of the Everett-Wheeler theory puts into

sharp relief the great originality of Jorge Louis Borges in anticipating the essentials of its concept of reality not under the prod-
ding stimulus of problems in natural philosophy but through the
sole exercise of creative imagination.[4]

5. SAVING THE LAW OF CONTRADICTION IN A BORGES WORLD

A Borges world of the sort envisaged by this Everett-Wheeler
theory obviously invites problems of consistency. It threatens to
violate the Law of Contradiction, for how can a single experiment possibly lead to divergent, logically incompatible but yet
equally real results. In different terms, how can the Borges
hypothesis be made compatible with our regulative acceptance
of the consistency of nature? How can the Law of Contradiction
be maintained in these circumstances?

There is only one possible way. Looking back to the Aristotelian
Law of Contradiction, one sees that it becomes necessary to
find—somewhere and somehow—a *difference of respect* between
the alternative but coordinate experimental outcomes conjointly
existing in one selfsame world.

The search for a resolution along these lines is facilitated by
reflecting on a comparable difficulty arising in the world-view
of the ancient Greek Atomists. They too held the view that every
(suitably general) possibility is realized in fact. Confronting the
question "Why do dogs not have horns: why is the possibility that
dogs be horned not realized?" the Atomists replied that it *is*
realized but simply *in another region of space*. Somewhere within
infinite space there is another world just like ours in every respect
save one, that dogs have horns. That dogs don't have horns is
simply a parochial idiosyncracy of the particular local world in
which we interlocutors happen to find ourselves. All alternative
possibilities are actualized in the various subworlds embraced
within one spatially infinite superworld.

On this Atomistic view the logical clash between conflicting
yet equally real alternatives is resolved by postulating a difference
of respect, namely in respect of location in space. Once such a
difference in respect is given, the Law of Contradiction is clearly

---

[4] For an excellent semipopular account of the Everett-Wheeler theory
see B. S. DeWitt, "Quantum Mechanics and Reality," *Physics Today*
(Sept., 1970), pp. 30–5.

saved: the conflicting cases will then not be alike in *every* respect.

In the world of ancient Atomists, consistency is salvaged by introducing a difference of respect in regard to space. The intriguing prospect arises that in a Borges world an essentially comparable solution becomes possible by introducing an analogous difference of respect in regard to *time*.

6. BRANCHING TIME AND MULTI-DIMENSIONAL HISTORY

One ordinarily thinks of time as a single one dimensional stream with different moments strung out like beads on a continuous string, a view which is enshrined in the standard physicists' picture of a "time axis":

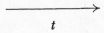

$$t$$

But suppose that time were not like this at all. Suppose that *time is a tree-like structure* with branches occurring at all junctures at which contingent events can be located, each branching point having as many branches going off from it as there are possible outcomes of the contingency:

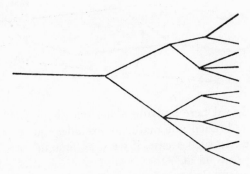

The working out of the logical details of such an, in effect, tree-like view of time as a branching structure is due to A. N. Prior.[5] Whenever a contingent event with diverse possible outcomes is envisaged, we are invited to consider time as itself splitting into a

---

[5] See A. N. Prior, *Time and Modality* (Oxford, 1957); *Past, Present, and Future* (Oxford, 1967).

H

plurality of distinct branches each accommodating one of the alternative outcomes.

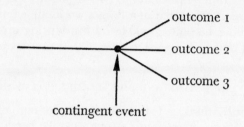

outcome 1

outcome 2

outcome 3

contingent event

Now there are two distinct and crucially different ways of viewing *the actual world* in terms of such a picture. If we specify the "world" in terms of its history, in terms of what *actually* happens in it, two very different pictures are possible. One is to take only one single track as real and to regard all others as unrealized alternatives. The history of the world—the account of its reality—consists in specifying what happens along one single branch

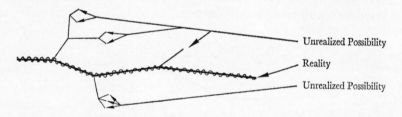

Unrealized Possibility

Reality

Unrealized Possibility

Reality is viewed here as lying along one single track, and the reality of one branch automatically excludes that of all alternative branches. In such a case, if we view time in terms of "what actually happens in it," then real time—the time of actually real occurrences—is once again simply linear. It is a one dimensional continuum embedded in a branching structure of unrealized (and so extra-temporal) alternatives, mapping out the alternative possible histories of one selfsame world. But an importantly different alternative position is to view reality as placed equally and uniformly along the entire system of tracks. On this view all of the various paths would be heavily shaded. This approach simply *cancels out* the whole realm of unrealized possibility: *all* alternative possibilities are alike real. Again, viewing time in terms of history—in terms of "what actually happens in it"—we obtain a genuinely branching structure. Time now is essentially two-dimensional.[6] It is no longer a matter of *variant* histories of a world whose reality is strung out along one dimensional time: the temporal history of the world is a branching picture of a complex reality embracing conflicting alternatives in a structurally ramified framework of time.[7] This requires us to assume a doubly nonstandard point of view. On the one hand, we view reality as a Borges world in which incompatible alternatives are conjointly realized. On the other hand, we view time as an essentially two-dimensional branching structure. And we effect a wedding between these two positions by mapping the world into the structure, stringing out the alternative realities along the divergent paths of time.

In viewing the time/reality complex in this manner as a genuinely branching structure we at once obtain the means for saving the Law of Contradiction in a Borges world. The seeming contradiction between conflicting yet supposedly equally real outcomes of a contingent situation are reconciled by introducing the requisite difference in respect: the alternatives differ in point of their placement within time. They occur, that is, not at different times, but at different but yet coordinated positions within the internally complex branching structure of time.

On this approach one is able to save the traditional Law of Contradiction even when adopting the Everett-Wheeler theory with its picture of quantum reality as a Borges world. The saving maneuver is to introduce the requisite "difference of respect" in temporal terms, by adopting the view of time as a branching structure.[8]

---

[6] See N. Rescher and A. Urquhart, *Temporal Logic* (New York and Vienna, 1971).

[7] I must "eat crow" regarding my earlier contention that the only natural interpretation of branching time was along the lines of the first interpretation. See N. Rescher and A. Urquhart, *ibid.*, pp. 70–4.

[8] One theoretical difficulty of the Everett-Wheeler theory has not, I think, been adequately resolved by its advocates. An actualistic treatment of *possibility* calls for a comparably actualistic treatment of *probability*. And this is seemingly available only along some such lines as the following, that if (for example) a stochastic process can lead to two

Interestingly enough, a resolution along essentially these lines was proposed by Borges himself in the short story under discussion:

I had questioned myself about the ways in which a book can be infinite. I could think of nothing other than a cyclic volume, a circular one. A book whose last page was identical with the first, a book which had the possibility of continuing indefinitely. . . . In the midst of this perplexity, I received from Oxford the manuscript you have examined. I lingered, naturally, on the sentence: *I leave to the various futures (not to all) my garden of forking paths.* Almost instantly, I understood: "the garden of forking paths" was the chaotic novel; the phrase "the various futures (not to all)" suggested to me the forking in time, not in space. A broad rereading of the work confirmed the theory. . . . *The Garden of Forking Paths* is an enormous riddle, or parable, whose theme is time. . . . In contrast to Newton and Schopenhauer. . . . [its author] did not believe in a uniform, absolute time. He believed in an infinite series of times, in a growing, dizzying net of divergent, convergent and parallel times. This network of times which approaches one another, forked, broke off, or were unaware of one another for centuries,

---

outcomes A and B, but with B twice as likely as A, then we have not only the two equi-actual paths

but rather three equi-actual paths

representing three distinct worlds. Two of these worlds (viz., the B-eventuating ones) are precisely alike. How such distinct worlds that are entirely indistinguishable can be envisaged is, to say the least a serious problem, familiar to philosophers in relation to the "Principle of the Identity of Indiscernibles." The apparent violation of this principle in a natural philosophy of the Everett-Wheeler type calls for a justifying rationale that has not, I think, as yet been provided.

embraces *all* possibilities of time. We do not exist in the majority of these times; in some you exist, and not I; in others I, and not you; in others, both of us. In the present one, which a favourable fate has granted me, you have arrived at my house; in another, while crossing the garden, you found me dead; in still another, I utter these same words, but I am a mistake, a ghost. . . . Time forks perpetually towards innumerable futures.[9]

As the man himself saw quite clearly, the Borges hypothesis points towards a nonstandard concept of time, one that views it as not linear, but a tree-like structure with a multiplicity of branches.

7. COULD WE ABANDON THE "LAW OF CONTRADICTION"?

We have tried to see how close one can skate to the dark depths of inconsistency; how far one can go in describing a world that contains self-contradictions. But, in the final analysis, such a Borges world in which actually incompatible alternatives are conjointly realized can be regained for the domain of consistency by going over to a nonstandard view of time. The day can be saved for logical consistency by postulating a branching time that is effectively two-dimensional. In this way, the Law of Contradiction has been restored to operation in a seemingly self-contradictory world. The question now remains: Could *anything* happen to force us into abandoning the Law of Contradiction. Or is it in principle impossible that a course of events should somehow move us away from our regulative maintenance of the Law of Contradiction in its tough Aristotelian formulation?

8. VARIANT LOGICS

With respect to this question it is perhaps tempting to the contemporary mind to reason as follows:

Various systems of deductive logic alternative to the traditional two-valued logic have been proposed in this century. Accordingly, it is possible that there should be some perfectly viable "alternative logic" in which the Law of Contradiction fails to obtain. Could not the course of events be such as to induce us to adopt such a non-

[9] J. L. Borges, *op. cit.*, pp. 51–3.

standard logic as "correct," thereby leading us to abandon the Law of Contradiction?

The issues posed by this line of thought are immensely complicated. I have dealt with them at some length in another place and can do no more than to sketch the upshot in somewhat rough and ready fashion.[10]

To begin with, it is necessary to be somewhat more precise as to just exactly what the so-called Law of Contradiction with which we are dealing actually says. Traditional logicians generally construed the Law of Contradiction to say that *nothing can be both A and non-A*, or, in a somewhat different formulation that "B is A" and "B is not-A" cannot both be true together—at least one member of the pair must be false. Certainly in the context of many-valued logic this "law" can take various distinct forms.[11] One of these versions, however, can plausibly be held to represent a strictly necessary relationship, to wit:

> The "exclusion principle" that a proposition (say, p) and its negation $(\sim p)$ cannot both be true together: at most one can be true, so that the truth of one excludes or precludes that of the other.

Certainly in this (very weak) form no known system of logic violates the principle. And for good reason. For if both "p" and " $\sim p$" were true, then one could scarcely maintain $\sim$ as a viable mode of negation.

Let us now return to the prospect of finding an alternative system of logic superior to the standard one and dispensing with the Law of Contradiction. It is well to begin here by reflecting a moment as to what sort of rational process this can be, this deciding that some essentially nonstandard system of logic is "a better system of deductive logic" than one of the sort standardly employed. The following steps are obviously necessary.

(1) one is given another system that conforms to the *basic defining conditions* of a system of deductive logic.
(2) one is given some *specification of the fundamental purposes* that such systems of deductive logic are to serve: they must provide a canon of rational inference, must be truth-pre-

[10] See N. Rescher, *Many-valued Logic* (New York, 1969).
[11] *Ibid.*, pp. 143–8.

serving (yield true conclusions for true premisses), etc.
(3) one then determines that the system under consideration in point (1) serves the purpose specified in point (2) better than systems of a more orthodox character.

Accordingly, one begins with a certain conceptually *defining basis* to determine what a "system of logic" is (an axiomatization of Euclidean geometry obviously won't do). And one evaluates alternatives within this previously determined family of "systems of deductive logic" by means of *purposive criteria*. The two factors of defining basis and purposive criteria are requisites fundamental to the whole line of thought that underlies the argument under consideration.

Now it is not only possible, but plausible, to maintain the thesis that satisfaction of the Law of Contradiction is part of the *defining basis* for a system violating this law—a system in which a proposition and its negation can both be true together—is simply not a system of logic, whatever else its merits might be. It would be viewed as one of the qualifying conditions for logical systems that they guarantee consistency. Satisfaction of this condition would be viewed as an essential component of the very concept of a "system of logic."

The resolution is possible and indeed plausible. It may very well be the right way of viewing the matter. I certainly can think of no convincing reason why it should not be. All the same, it strikes me as perhaps a little too *ex cathedra*. Though it is difficult to dismiss it as incorrect, this *constitutive* way of seeing the place of the Law of Contradiction as part of the determinative defining basis for systems of logic is possibly too pat a solution.

The path I prefer to follow, because I regard it as an intellectually more comfortable alternative, is to obtain the Law of Contradiction from the purposive criteria for logical systems. It would accordingly be maintained that a proposed system of deductive logic just could not serve the characterizing purposes of such systems if it did not satisfy the Law of Contradiction. That is, no system of logic that tolerated the concurrent truth of a proposition and its negation could answer to the purposes for which such systems are instituted within the framework of rational inquiry. Accordingly, the principle is seen as essentially *regulative* in status.

If one takes this line of approach and views the Law of Contradiction as inherent in the purposively regulative criteria for systems of logic, then it is *inevitable* that the question with which we began—"Might some alternative system of logic superior to the standard system not dispense with the Law of Contradiction?"—will be answered in the negative. It is necessary—but now not *definitionally* necessary but *purposively* necessary—that the Law of Contradiction should hold in whatever system of logic we adopt as appropriate.

One point of nagging doubt must be laid to rest. This is posed by the question: Is it not possible that one might simply *change* the purposively regulative criteria for systems of logic in such a way that the Law of Contradiction no longer emerges from them?

The answer is: No! In a broader (or looser) sense, the purposive criteria are *just as essential* to our concept of logic as the conditions of the defining basis. To change the purposes is to change the rules by which the whole game is played. To alter the purposes is as serious as to alter the defining conditions—in either case we simply "change the subject" and deal no longer with logic construed along the generally understood lines. To change the purposive criteria specific to systems of deductive logic is to depart from talking of such systems as we understand them and to go on to talk of different matters. Accordingly, the Law of Contradiction would not be viewed as *definitionally* necessary for a *system of logic* as such—in the sense of being part of the very definition of the concept. Yet this law would nonetheless constitute an inevitable feature of such a system within the purposive framework of this intellectual dispensation.

On this approach, then, the purpose-oriented basis on which the Law of Contradiction rests moves into view in sharper outline. We come to see the regulative role of the principle as inherent not in the descriptive features of the world as revealed by rational inquiry into the workings of nature, but in the goals and procedural mechanisms of inquiry that we ourselves bring to the task. Accordingly, the principle assumes the status of a necessity that is not categorical, but hypothetical, because rooted in the functional goal-structure of human purpose. And at this, its crucial juncture, the Kantian route of analysis takes a decisively pragmatic or instrumentalistic turn.

9. CONCLUSION

In bringing this perhaps too wide-ranging discussion to its end, it seems useful to restate its principal contentions briefly. The first point was that the self-consistency of nature is not a *constitutive* principle characterizing the internal constitution of nature as such, but a *regulative* principle relating to our procedures for its conceptualization. We then maintained that the traditional Aristotelian Law of Contradiction can be supported on exactly the same basis, its appropriateness being attributed to our conceptualization of reality, that is, as a regulative principle for its intellectual rationalization. It would thus be a definitely misleading oversimplification to attribute this self-consistency directly to the nature of reality as such. Man did not at some historical juncture discover through extensive observation or elaborate experiment that the world is self-consistent—nor yet by theorizing on such a basis—and one could not in principle so discover in the future that it is not. The consistency of nature is *a product of ultimately regulative features of the conceptual apparatus we deploy for its rationalization.* (The ultimate validation of this apparatus is pragmatic and Darwinian in nature, and so it could, in theory, be given up on grounds of *this* character. But this sort of vulnerability does not affect its security from specifically empirical findings.)

The regulative status of the principle of the consistency of nature marks it as resting on a basis that is not empirical but a priori *vis-à-vis* our information-providing-experience. The rational controls operative in its legitimation are accordingly pragmatic rather than evidential: its validating rationale lies ultimately in the practical rather than the cognitive sphere. It affords yet a further example of the subordination of theoretical to practical reason in the context of the foundations of our empirical knowledge.

This all-out support for the Law of Contradiction as a regulative principle might on first thought seem to conflict with a conception that has made headlines in recent physics, the idea of the Everett-Wheeler theory that nature might be so complex that its reality has the character of a Borges world in embracing logically conflicting alternatives. We have contended that—first appearances notwithstanding—the traditional Law of Contradiction can in fact be restored in such an inconsistency-containing Borges world by embedding the complex of occurrences of such a world in a system of branching time.

Peace can thus be made between the Everett-Wheeler theory and the Aristotelian Law of Contradiction by following the lead of Borges and Prior in making suitable resort to an essentially two-dimensional concept of time as a branching structure. In *this* particular regard at least—and other cases might, of course, eventuate differently—an extremely radical physics can be combined with an emphatically conservative logic.

Chapter VI

A CRITIQUE OF PURE ANALYSIS

1. THE PURISTS' VIEW OF CONCEPTUAL ANALYSIS

The purists among the practitioners of conceptual analysis in philosophy have always looked to logic and mathematics as their ideal. They see the task of conceptual analysis as illuminating the outer boundaries and inner articulations of concepts by heeding solely their logico-semantical relationships to one another. The professed aim is to clarify and precisify the anatomical structure of the concepts we standardly use in our everyday, our philosophical, and our scientific talk about the world with the same abstract exactitude and precision that one customarily encounters in the logico-mathematical realm. The enterprise falls heir to the legacy of Descartes as regards his search for clear and distinct ideas to be apprehended by a mind emptied of the clutter of empirical fact and placing exclusive reliance on the illuminative power of the light of reason. Accordingly, the practitioners of pure analysis see the relationships among concepts as "purely conceptual" in nature (it seems virtually redundant to say it), and therefore as fixed by wholly *a priori* and strictly semantical considerations, without any reference to extra-conceptual, empirical fact. Throughout this venture, the dual aspect of the *precision* and the *necessity* of wholly abstract conceptual inter-relationships is placed in the foreground.

This perspective accounts for the methodological lure that puzzle-cases seemingly have for many discussions in analytic philosophy. The pursuit of conceptual clarity and precision makes it tempting to drive our concepts against the scalpel's edge of hypothetical cases that require sharp-edged and clearly articulated resolutions to bring their semantical anatomy to view.[1]

---

[1] One can invoke on this head the authority of Bertrand Russell, one of the founding fathers of the enterprise:

> A logical theory may be tested by its capacity for dealing with puzzles, and it is a wholesome plan, in thinking about logic [and Russell here intends logical analysis in general throughout the philosophical arena], to stock the mind with as many puzzles as possible, since these serve much the same purpose as is served by experiments in physical science. (*Mind*, vol. 14 [1905] pp. 484–485.)

The prominence of this methodological tendency of dwelling upon puzzle-cases is readily substantiated by examples that give a kind of science-fiction aspect to much of the philosophizing of this tradition. Accordingly, the discourse of analytical philosophers is full of intelligent robots and strikingly gifted men from outer space, dream/waking interchanges, brain-transplants and personality transmigrations, amnesia victims with perfect recall of other peoples' past, uncannily accurate precognition, and the like. The view seems to be that extraordinary cases are conductive to precision, and that the workings of our concepts are most clearly illuminated by seeing how they comport themselves in the context of far-out suppositions.

2. DIFFICULTIES OF ANALYTICAL PURISM

Unfortunately, however, with many concepts of philosophically central interest, this seemingly attractive road of analytical purism leads straightaway into difficulties of a special and characteristic type. Let me illustrate this with respect to the conception of certain phenomena as "objectively real" rather than being illusions or delusions or the like. As one reflects upon an appraisal of the *objective reality* of phenomena, it comes to notice that distinct considerations are pivotally important here, in that the determination of the objective reality of an experience involves a variety of determinants, a plurality of two key members which are the factors of *lawfulness* (i.e., observed regularity, cohesiveness with the general course of environing phenomena) and *consensus* (i.e., accord with the reported experience of others). Both of these appear to enter crucially into our standard concept of "a phenomenon that is objectively real." And by and large we are quite prepared to take either one as sufficiently indicative. One cannot, of course, avoid the recognition that there is no *logical* linkage here. The two factors can in principle wander off on their separate ways. We can readily hypothesize on the one hand an experientially isolated prodigy (a person whose *utterly systematic* experiences all others view as being idiosyncratic), and on the other a person who inhabits an experiental chaos in that his noncommunicative experience is highly irregular, though he is in consensus with his fellows as to its nature. In the abstract logic of the case there is no reason *of principle* why the authenticity-determining factors of lawfulness and consensus—which our concept of objectivity treats as standardly coordinated—should inevitably have to go together. But *in fact* our concept is such that the contrast between authentic and delusory experience operative in our idea of objective reality construes this as a *fusion* of phenomenological detail (force and vivacity, detail, depth), internal manifest orderliness and systematic, contextual regularity (lawfulness, coherence), and concurrence with the reported experience of others.

Accordingly, an analytical purist would seek to assist us in "making up our mind" as to which of these two factors is decisive, or if both separate items should prove conjointly required to determine just what their relative roles and contributions are within that complex mixture in which they must both be co-present.

Now it is not difficult to see that in the case in hand—and a vast family of others for which it is paradigmatic—we just cannot do this: we cannot make a neat ruling as to what relative contribution of conceptual weight is to be carried by each one of several factors linked together in one of our common concepts. What goes wrong here? Are such ordinary concepts just plain sloppy in some logico-sentimental sense? Is their "rational reconstruction" called for? I shall begin by arguing that *this* orienting of an analytical approach to such concepts barks up the wrong philosophical tree.

3. FACT-COORDINATIVE CONCEPTS

Many of the concepts we standardly use in our thoughts regarding the arrangements of this world are of essentially *composite* character. Rather than representing a fusion of diverse conceptual elements whose coming together is underwritten by purely conceptual and semantical relationships, *the concurrence basic to the concept rests on a strictly empirical foundation*. This is true in particular of various philosophically central ideas.

A few examples may clarify this abstract point:

(1) PERSONAL IDENTITY as implementing a concept of the sameness of persons that is a fusion of *bodily continuity*

(tracking through space and time) and *continuity of personality* (memory, habits, tastes, dispositions, skills, etc.). (Moreover, each of these is itself composite.)

(2) PERSONS as coordinated joinings of *mind* and *body*, and a mutually accordant functioning of mental and bodily activity, thus manifesting two very different sets of characteristic powers and dispositions.

(3) VALUE (in the sense of "social justice is one of his values") as involving a fusion of three sorts of factors: covert ("mentalistic" thought, motivation, rationalization), transitional (verbal behavior in affording *vis-à-vis* others some defense, explanation, or justification of one's acts), and overt (actual physical behavior).

(4) BELIEF as a fusion of mentalistic dispositions to think and overt dispositions to action.

Note that all of these various philosophically critical concepts are both multicriterial and fact-coordinative:

(i) They are *multicriterial* because in each case a plurality of in principle separable components enter in (e.g., in the personal identity case both bodily continuity and continuity of personality).

(ii) They are *fact-coordinative* because in each case the theoretically separable but concept-joined criterial factors are held together in an integrative fusion by facts or purported facts (i.e., by a view of how the world actually works). (Thus in the personal identity case we find that bodily continuity and continuity of personality generally and standardly *go together*.)

Let just one of these concepts serve as a detailed example—say *belief*. Note that both key factors at issue here (mentalistic disposition and overt behavior) must come together before it is proper to speak of "believing." His mental state alone won't do to establish that X believes that a bomb is shortly to go off in the room if his every act belies this (under suitable circumstances —e.g., he has no wish to commit suicide). But evasion-behavior alone won't clinch the matter either, if there is sufficient evidence that X's every thought—tacit and professed—indicates in every conceivable way that he is nowise under an impression that a bomb is present. All of the appropriate facts must be co-present before we can unproblematically speak of X's belief. Otherwise we could not appropriately say purely and simply that X believes that P, but would have to use some suitably complex circumlocution, "X, while not accepting that P is the case, acts as though it were," "X, though maintaining that P is the case, certainly does not behave in an accordant fashion," or the like.

In nonstandard cases some such circumlocution is always called for. In the standard cases—the only ones where the concept in view is *unproblematically* applicable—the various criterial factors (thought, profession, and action in the belief case) must work together. And the very viability of the concept in view—its ability to function as the concept it is—hinges on the *empirical* fact that what is characterized as "the standard case" is actually generally realized (in the belief case that the world is such that peoples' thoughts, professions, and actions will usually and standardly cohere). At the base of such a concept, then, lies an empirically underwritten coordination that places the various critical factors into a symbiotic, mutually supportive relationship. Accordingly, the concept is fact-coordinated in exactly this respect of envisaging a coming-together of theoretically distinct factors whose union is itself the product not of conceptual necessity but of empirical fact.

In such cases, of which the handful adduced here are but illustrative instances, I am concerned to maintain a specific version of the more or less trite and familiar proposition that our concepts are in general theory-presupposing. However, it appears that a very special sort of theory is to be at issue here, namely a theory whose import is *coordinative* or—to use the word in its root sense—*conspiratorial*; that is to say one to the effect that, things being as they are, certain factors always or standardly work together in communal co-presence.

Concepts of this fact-coordinative sort rest on presuppositions whose content is factual, reflecting a view of how things go in the world. Such concepts are developed and deployed against a fundamentally empirical backdrop, a Weltanschauung, or rather some miniscule sector thereof. The crucial contribution of such a theory is to produce the result that in suitable cases of the conjoining of a plurality of factors that are in principle separable from one another, we are *spared any need to make up our mind* as to which of the plurality of factors involved is ultimately determinative or decisive.[2]

In the interests of exactness it is worthwhile to lay out the abstract anatomy of the situation. We are dealing with a fundamentally *multicriterial* concept C, with respect to which a series of logical distinct criterial factors F_1, F_2, ..., F_n can be articulated. The pivotal consideration is that in this, the actual world, these F_i in fact go together so as to be *fact-coordinative*:

$$F_i \leftrightarrow F_j \ (i, j = 1, 2, \ldots, n)$$

Accordingly, no difficulty arises with respect to a concept C governed by the family of meaning-postulates:

$$C \leftrightarrow F_i$$

Because of their (admittedly contingent) coincidence, the F_i can join together to underwrite the viability of this thesis-family as a basis for working of the concept C in this, the actual world. But once we introduce hypotheses to disassemble the realm of actual truth we also dismantle the scaffolding of contingent fact on which the concept rests. Insisting on the logical distinctness of the F_i, and supposing the actualization of their possible divergence, we no longer have the single and unified concept C as initially constituted, but rather obtain a vast series of alternatives:

$$C_1 \leftrightarrow F_1$$
$$-$$
$$-$$
$$-$$
$$C_n \leftrightarrow F_n$$
$$C_{i,\,j} \leftrightarrow F_i \ \& \ F_j$$
$$C_{1,\,2,\,\ldots,\,n} \leftrightarrow F_1 \ \& \ F_2 \ \& \ \ldots \ \& \ F_n$$

Note incidentally that the last of these, though superficially like our initial C, is in fact profoundly different from it. For if we accepted it as the determinative rule, the C-like version it provides is no longer a concept X such that $F_i \leftrightarrow X$, and so differs decisively from C. The point that on *this* C-version obtains its definitional tidiness by having all of the F_i as separately necessary

---

[2] The key fact is not that nature takes a benign view of our *a priori* preconceptions, but that our concepts develop within the processes of nature in ways shaped by processes of Darwinian selection.

but only jointly sufficient conditions of applicability, whereas the original C was based on the view that when one of the F_i was present, the rest could all be "taken for granted," so that the various F_i are already in themselves separately sufficient. The two articulations point in different directions. The one concept calls for an *explicit* conjoining of conditions, and accordingly applies in *all* possible worlds; the other is operative only in those cases where certain conditions are conjoined, and accordingly is implicitly limited in its application to those possible worlds where these conditions are met. The factor-coordinative concept is fundamentally different from its factor-conjunctive cousin in its import. Where the one has an explicit condition for its application the other has an implict condition of definition or meaningfulness.

The crucial fact is that a concept may be woven around a family of "meaning postulates" (that is, principles governing the semantical conditions of its use) which embody relationships that obtain as a matter of contingent fact. When hypotheses are introduced with the effect of abrogating these underlying facts, then any prospect of maintaining the concept itself is annihilated, because the very content of that concept rests on an empirical presupposition that has been violated.

4. SOME CONSEQUENCES FOR CONCEPTUAL ANALYSIS

The remainder of the chapter will be devoted to tracing out some of the philosophically germane consequences of a recognition that certain key concepts maintain their integrity on a basis of fact or purported fact, with the result that their viability is factually conditional.

The most obvious of these consequences relates to the methodology of conceptual analysis itself—at any rate when such empirically conditioned, fact-coordinating concepts are at issue. For in such cases, it comes to be in principle impossible that the analysis could be *pure*. When the very meaning-content of a concept is fact-presupposing, then its analysis cannot—in the very nature of the case—operate on the strictly semantical level of the inner logic of concepts, proceeding in abstraction from all empirical considerations, without any reference to empirical matters of fact. Accordingly, the analyst must take care not to press his would-be clarification beyond the cohesive force of the

I

factual considerations that hold together the concept as such. And this has definite implications regarding the usability of the science-fiction type of thinking in which—as we have remarked —analytic philosophers frequently delight.

The literature of the philosophy of mind is full of personality exchanges between people (which one is the "same person"?) and robots whose communicative behavior is remarkably anthropoidal (are they "conscious" or not?). But if my analysis of the conceptual situation is anything like correct, such proceedings are intrinsically defective. The assumptions at issue call for the suppositional severing of things that normally go together in circumstances where the concepts we use are predicated upon a certain background of "normality." An analytically clarificatory hypothesis must not cut asunder what the basic facts of this world have joined together—at any rate not where those concepts whose life-blood is drawn from the source of fact are concerned. To force a concept into a mold shaped by hypothetical assumptions under which its characteristic conditions of operation are abrogated, does not *clarify* this concept but rather *distorts* it. The result will not be the same concept only in sharpened form, but an actually different concept or set of concepts—one whose problems and issues we cannot resolve in the same language. Such a distortion does not produce a *sharpening* of the concepts in view, but leads to their *abandonment*: it does not clarify but rather replaces the initial concepts with which we began, and while various considerations may warrant such a replacement, the interests of the clarification of *existing* concepts cannot be among them.

If the normality-violating hypothesis is radical, then our normalcy-envisioning concepts cannot be brought to bear at all. We have no glib reply to the question "What would you say if . . . (if worst came to worst [e.g., if flowers started talking like people])?" When the hypothetical upheaval is sufficiently radical we have to go through the agonizingly innovative process of rebuilding part of our conceptual scheme from the ground up. Genuine conceptual innovation is necessary and there is no way of predicting its outcome. To the question "What would you say if . . .?" we would in such cases have to reply: "We just wouldn't know what to say . . . We'll just have to cross that bridge when we get there."

The project of construing a concept along clearer lines by the introduction of outré science-fiction examples can prove a myth based on an illusion. From the perspective of our standard framework of fact-presupposingly multicriterial concepts, the actual result will be confusion instead of clarity when an hypothesis abrogates the background understanding of how things work in the world that is an indispensable foundation for such concepts.[3]

From this standpoint, the fundamentally fact-dependent nature of our conceptual apparatus is a consideration of great relevance for philosophical inquiry. Our concepts can and generally do develop against the background of an understanding of "how things work" in the world (or better, "are taken by us to work"); they are tied to a view of the realities of nature and to the empirical detail of actually existing practices. If we introduce hypotheses to abrogate these "underlying realities," the foothold for our concepts dissolves and the relevant sector of our conceptual scheme simply goes up in smoke. It would go too far to say that no useful purpose whatsoever can be realized in this way. For example, a science-fiction hypothesis can effectively bring to light the significant fact *that* certain of our concepts are indeed multicriterial and rest on empirical presuppositions. But what this method cannot do is to serve as a basis for precisifying our *existing* concepts, because the supposedly more precise account that results in these circumstances will not and in the nature of the case cannot any longer qualify as a version of the concept with which we began.

The point of these observations is not to advocate an unbudging conservatism in the conceptual area. No doubt there

[3] Thus W. V. Quine is to my mind entirely right when he objects: "[In Schoemaker's discussion of Wiggins on personal identity] the reasoning veers off in familiar fashion into speculation on what we might say in absurd situations of cloning and transplanting. The method of science fiction has its uses in philosophy, but at points in the Schoemaker-Wiggins exchange and elsewhere I wonder whether the limits of the method are properly heeded. To seek what is 'logically required' for sameness of person under unprecedented conditions is to suggest that words have some logical force beyond what our past needs have invested them with." (Review of M. K. Munitz [ed.], *Identity and Individuation* in *The Journal of Philosophy*, vol. 69 [1972], pp. 488–97 [see p. 490].) Our present discussion in effect attempts to explore just where "the limits of the method" lie.

might conceivably be substantial advantages to giving up some of our concepts in favor of others. But such conceptual innovation has no *intrinsic* advantages that make it attractive for its own sake. It is only to be done on the basis of a careful cost-benefit analysis of its relative advantages and drawbacks *vis-à-vis* the given architecture of our existing concepts.

Now with the sorts of fact-coordinating concepts we have in view (mind, person, appearance/reality), a special consideration arises in this cost-benefit assessment. For many such concepts are pivotal to the tradition of philosophical inquiry in which we work. And to abandon them in favor of other concepts will— no matter how appealing or delightful its advantages and attractions may seem—have at least this serious drawback, that in abandoning these concepts we quit the traditional arena of philosophical discussion: we simply "take our marbles and go home." And whatever appeal this step may have, it is not one that we can take *within* the framework of the professed objective of a clarificatory analysis of philosophical issues. It is scarcely candid to pass off the wolf of abandonment as the sheep of clarification. And it is surely a mistaken procedure to practice conceptual "clarification" in such a manner as to destroy the very items we are purportedly clarifying.

5.   THE KANTIAN ASPECT: ANTINOMIES

A fundamental analogy with the Kantian ethic of universalization is at work here in regard to our fact coordinative concepts. For Kant, one could not—without havoc to moral concepts—coherently assume that a practice in violation of moral norms should be the standard, because this restandardization would destroy the very practice at issue. (If we assume—for example—that people by and large break promises, then the whole practice of promise-giving as it actually exists would become unviable.) On our view, one could not coherently—without havoc to factually based concepts—assume that a condition of things in violation of a concept-coordinating generalization should be the standard, because this restandardization would destroy the very concept at issue. (If we assume—for example—that people's thoughts and actions by and large diverged from one another, then our whole concept of belief as it actually exists would become unworkable because of the violence done to its essential factual presupposition.) In either case, if one assumes a systematic alteration of the underlying regularity, then the initial item (a practice in the one case, a concept in the other) is destroyed. This Kantian analogy may seem somewhat incidental, but this reaction is erroneous. Let us explore somewhat more deeply the fundamentally Kantian ramifications of this entire approach.

The preceding discussion has probed the reasons why an analytical sharpening of fact-coordinating concepts must not press them beyond the cohesive capacity of the facts that by uniting their logico-semantically disparate elements into a cohesive unit, make them viable as the concepts they are. At present I want briefly to consider the consequences that ensue if we actually persist in exerting such pressure in defiance of these reasons.

For the moment, let us proceed by means of examples. Take personal identity. As noted above, this concept unites a plurality of factors among which bodily continuity and sameness of personality are the outstanding members, factors held together in a harmonious symbiosis by *factual* considerations. Suppose that, in the interests of eliminating the empirical element and obtaining semantical tidyness we put all of our conceptual eggs into one basket, and take one of these factors as essential, the other as accidental. Thus let us adopt bodily continuity as essential and relegate continuity of personality to the background. Immediately some clever doubter will pop up to construct a counter-example that cannot but make us uncomfortable with this choice. By mooting some fiendish electronic rewiring of their brain circuitry he will have Messrs A and B exchange personality characteristics: knowledge and memory, performatory capabilities, talents, inclinations, dispositions, etc., etc. Nothing is to remain the same except the lumps of material stuff. And now our objector protests: "According to your thesis that bodily continuity is the determining criterion, we should have no hesitancy in the case I have sketched about saying that we are dealing with the same person both before and after the personality exchange. But we unquestionably do feel a very considerable hesitancy. So this analysis that sees bodily continuity as decisive cannot be right." There seems to be much justification in this complaint. So let us try the opposite resolution, taking sameness of personality as determinative, and bodily continuity as incidental. At once another objector comes along with a different counterexample. He has one person so changed that all of his personality characteristics have altered over the course of a month or two, while someone else's personality has become far more like what his used to be. And then he protests "According to your thesis that similarity of personality is the key criterion of personal identity, we should have no hesitancy about saying in such a case that the personality-altered individual is no longer the same person, and it would become moot to consider whether our subject individual has metamorphosed into his simulacrum. But we would actually hesitate very much about saying this sort of thing. So bodily continuity is in fact the decisive criterion."

The implications of the two cases are diametrically opposed. And the crucial point is that quite evidently we are reluctant to live with the consequences of either resolution, because a ruling in favor of the primacy of any one of the fact-coordinated plurality of criteria does violence to our intuitive assessment of those cases where the other criteria come into predominating prominence. The arguments for and against each resolution are evenly or substantially balanced; we can always construct pretty much equally good arguments either way. In short, we fall into an antinomy.

The case is precisely analogous with the other sorts of concepts we have had in view. Take belief: if behavior is to be crucial, we hypothesize a man whose thoughts point in the wrong direction; if the mentalistic aspect is to be crucial we hypothesize someone whose actions—including verbal actions—go systematically in the counterindicated way. Take moral credit: if consequences are to be determinative, we hypothesize someone whose intentions are evil but frustrated; if intentions are to be pivotal, we hypothesize a man whose intentions are of the best as he goes about systematically working havoc all around.

There is no use prolonging this listing; the general pattern is by now clear enough. All of our standard fact-coordinative concepts exhibit an inner semantical tension due to the plurality of their constituent components. This inner stress among logically divergent factors is standardly resolved by the favorable cooperation of empirical circumstance: the tension is unproblematic because the facts (as we see them) are duly cooperative. But once we give up our reliance on these facts in the interests of semantical neatness, the tension breaks out. For when we set the facts aside, the concept at issue itself disappears in a destructive fission. This disintegration manifests itself through opposing arguments—all seemingly equally good, but all in the final analysis equally unsatisfying. In consequence, what appears on first view as conceptual tidyness in making an ordinary concept more precise, results in a paradox-generating clash with the initial concept as it actually works, based as it is upon a unification in which the other, relegated factors are no less prominent. The antinomies that result are the inevitable indicators of this inner fission implicit in our fact-coordinative concepts.

6. THE ROLE OF AN EMPIRICAL FOUNDATION

I have maintained that many concepts of pivotal philosophical interest are theory-laden in that they represent a factually underwritten combination of logically diverse components, an empirically based coordination of theoretically distinct elements. This factual coordination is inseparably linked to a view of how things work in the world. And once we abstract from this view and introduce assumptions by which these factual links are abrogated, then we fall into antinomies whenever we seek to accommodate these strange cases by what seems on the surface no more than a called-for "clarification" of the concept in question.

Let us now re-examine this position from a more deeply Kantian perspective. Kant's basic thesis is that we cannot legitimately apply our concepts outside the limits of *possible experience*, and that when we do so we reach the intellectually unstable result of falling into antinomies. For Kant, the applicability of our concepts is validated through a categorical synthesis that renders them viable only when deployed *within* their area of valid employment: the domain of *possible* experience.

Our own position is closely analogous although critically different. We have made a crucial departure from Kant by replacing his *a priori* synthesis inherent in the faculty-structure of the human mind by a less ambitious but (I think) no less far-reachingly important reliance on the *empirical* synthesis built into a *Weltanschauung*, or some sector thereof. Accordingly, for us also, certain philosophical critical concepts are seen as usable only within "the limits of possible experience"—but *possible experience* now means *empirically* possible—i.e., possible relative to the empirical realities of a view of how things work in the world—that is, *actually* possible and not, as with Kant *transcendentally* possible. Our position, though Kantian in its fundamental structure, replaces his conceptual necessity by a more modest factual counterpart.

7.   IMPLICATIONS FOR PHILOSOPHICAL METHOD

In approaching the end of this discussion, I should like to set out some of its main conclusions.

Basic to the entire line of thought is the view that many concepts of philosophically central interest are collage-like: they are internally diversified *combinations* of logically separable elements that are held together by the glue of a theoretical view of the empirical facts. Such concepts rest in an essential way on an empirically based, fact-laden vision of how things work in the world.

One immediately arrives at a recognition of the impossibility of a neat separation between analytic and empirical truths when the analysis of such fact-coordinative concepts is at issue. With these concepts, semantical and factual considerations become intertwined: pure analysis can at best sort them out—it can bring the fact-invoking aspect of the concept to light, but it can in no way mitigate or remove this empirical aspect. With fact-coordinating concepts we are carried back to something approaching a theory of synthetic *a priori* truths. For not merely the *applicability* but even the very *viability* of these concepts calls for realization of certain empirical circumstances.

The existence of such an empirical background for our conceptual scheme accordingly has far-reaching philosophical ramifications. It means that our concepts are not framed to suit *every possible* world but in significant measure adjusted to *this* one. And, accordingly, seemingly analytic conceptual relations may actually reflect contingent facts, so that factual and conceptual considerations do not fall into neatly divided compartments. (Such inseparability of empirical from logico-conceptual considerations represents a central and ongoing theme of the Hegelian tradition that was by no means a latter-day invention of the author of "Two Dogmas of Empiricism.")

The main result of our discussion is, however, a methodological lesson relating to the process of philosophical analysis.

Insofar as one's philosophical concerns are—as many analysts have repeatedly proclaimed—*descriptive* and not *revisionary* of the standard conceptual scheme (in P. F. Strawson's sense of these terms), one must be careful about using the method of science-fiction examples for clarificatory purposes. One should not press these concepts into theoretical dichotomies that subject them to stresses they cannot bear. The key methodological lesson to emerge from these considerations seems to me to be this: that IF we are serious about the descriptive clarification of the way in which we standardly use certain philosophically central concepts, THEN we cannot shirk the task of investigating also the "view of reality" that underlies them and provides their indispensable foundation. And this inquiry is in significant measure empirical and *not* purely semantico-analytical. Their fact-reflecting character has the upshot that many key components of our "standard conceptual scheme" represent a constellation of logically and semantically separable and separate items held together in a cohesive unity by empirical facts (i.e., by "the way the world is" or rather "the way we think the world is"). These concepts are accordingly theory-based in a way that leads our conceptual scheme to reflect a vision of reality that must be brought to light if they are genuinely to be "clarified." And thus one cannot genuinely advance the analytical cause of "conceptual clarification" in a way that separates "conceptual analysis" from an empirical inquiry into something like a sociology of *Weltanschauungen*. The project of a *pure* conceptual analysis of our philosophically central concepts, viewed as a program wholly free of all empirical involvements, rests on a very questionable basis.

Something of a reformation in our programmatic attitude towards philosophical analysis is thus indicated. Many practitioners of conceptual clarification assume a disdainful attitude towards "mere matters of fact"—they see themselves as dealing with the "logic of concepts" in a pure, aprioristic manner, concerned to look to abstract relationships holding *sub specie aeternitatis* and dealing with conceptual issues quite in the abstract, independently of any factual considerations.

Insofar as our analysis of the philosophically prominent role of fact-coordinating concepts is correct, this view cannot be maintained. It becomes necessary to reject the thesis—so prominent in some quarters—that one automatically ceases "to do philosophy" once one begins to take account of empirical considerations. Anyone who is genuinely concerned with the philosophical elucidation of concepts as we actually use them must bear in mind that our conceptual scheme is not an abstract logicians' tool designed to deal with the endless ramifications of an infinite sphere of possible worlds; it is the product of an historically definite evolution within one specific and concretely real setting, and is accordingly such that its viability is at key places linked indissolubly to the experienced realities of this actual world.

These remarks are by no means to be regarded as a criticism of philosophical analysis *per se.* My objection is not at all directed against the method as such, but rather against what I view as the sort of *malpractice* that can degrade an intrinsically valuable technique. A proper practice of conceptual analysis can surely clarify how our concepts do in fact work and—when appropriate —render explicit their dependency upon facets of our view of the world. This calls for an endeavor to study concepts *in situ* with a view also to the empirical commitment that underwrites their use. The resulting study would heed the functional ecology of concepts, concerning itself not with semantics alone, but with the factual views operative within the common habitat of their standard employment.

Such a modest mission, with its preparedness to take notice of empirical realities, is probably not relished by most philosophical analysts, and certainly not by the purists among them. They tend to see themselves as pure theoreticians, concerned, like mathematicians and logicians, to clean up our ordinary and sloppy-seeming conceptions and deal with eternal truths. From the very outset, philosophers have been loath to come to grips with the empirical details of transient circumstances, aspiring to deal with timeless truths. Against this background a recognition that their concerns may in significant measure be consequent upon empirical inquiry as to how things work in the world—or even as socio-cultural-historical inquiry as to how people *think* things work— will doubtless seem a comedown. Still, realism would appear to require a critical view of the thesis (so near and dear to the hearts of many analytic philosophers) that philosophy can be altogether autonomous of the empirical sector. For in some of the central regions of the subject this ideal appears on closer scrutiny as altogether implausible.

8. THE PRAGMATIC ASPECT

The preceding discussion has maintained that various concepts of central philosophical interest are inseparably linked (in the very conceptual articulation that makes them what they are) to a view of "how things work in the world." On this approach, it certainly remains one of the key tasks of philosophy to provide for the critical evaluation of such concepts. But how can their criticism and evaluation be conducted? Of course, once a *variant* point of view regarding how things work in the world is given—one that is alien and external to the one initially at issue—then criticism is at once possible in terms of agreement or disagreement of the position at issue with that which is accepted as "canonical." But if it is our own seriously espoused view that is *internally* at issue, then this tactic is clearly infeasible. Now the answer cannot be given in terms of a standard of factual correctness as defined in terms of an agreement with some externally established position. Rather it must be sought internally, in the essentially pragmatic terms of their efficacious application in practice. On this view, the enterprise of philosophical critique of our fact-coordinated concepts is feasible, but must proceed, not in the *a priori* terms of theoretical correctness but rather in the *a posteriori* terms of pragmatic efficacy. The philosophical appraisal of factually-based conceptual schemes is a matter not for theoretical, but for essentially pragmatic analysis.[4]

---

[4] In writing this chapter I have benefited from the criticisms of my colleague Richard M. Gale upon an earlier version.

Chapter VII

THE EXTRA-PRAGMATIC DIMENSION OF HUMAN PURPOSE

I. INTRODUCTION

The tendency of the preceding chapters has been to indicate that practical purposes are the controlling norms for theory in the area of our empirical knowledge of contingent fact, and to maintain the primacy of practice in this factual domain. The question naturally arises whether this fundamentality of practice applies also in the normative areas as well as the informative. Are practical goals as determinative with respect to our judgements regarding values as with respect to those regarding facts? An at least brief exploration of this issue is the aim of these final chapters, which will endeavor to maintain that the primacy of practice does *not* carry over into the normative sphere, and to show why this is so.

The task of this chapter is to argue that the pragmatic domain of purpose aimed at man's welfare, happiness, and affective rewards is only a partial and incomplete subregion of the wider domain of valid human purpose in general, which also includes the, as it were, "higher," practicalities-transcending forms of human satisfaction. This point is crucially important for our wider position because it shows that the specifically pragmatic technique of justificating validation *is only one incomplete part* of the wider strategy of purposive or instrumental validation. The reader for whom these contentions constitute no difficulty, to whom it is pretty well self-evident that there are legitimate human purposes that lie altogether outside the practical sphere, is invited to pass this chapter by, and to proceed immediately to the one that follows.

2. THE SCOPE OF HUMAN PURPOSE

Human purposes fall into two groups, somewhat along the lines of the classical distinction between necessities and luxuries. The one category of purpose relates to the essentials of human welfare: to the strictly *practical goals* that have to do with the material interests of man, with what is needed to make life not only minimally possible, but even satisfactory. Throughout this first category we have to do with the hedonic dimension as it relates to the material interests of man not just in regard to the biomedical aspect of what makes life possible, but also the economic aspect of what makes life pleasant in terms of the availability of goods and services. The governing concept in this area of basic needs comprises those factors that relate to man's *welfare*.

The second category of purpose relates to the transcendent concerns of man in matters that lie outside the range of his material requirements for food, shelter, clothing, goods, services, etc., and so go beyond the economic area and the whole sphere of "enjoyment." Here we have to do not with man's needs for the basic requisites of a satisfactory life but with his enhanced desires for a life that is rewarding and meaningful. Not only happy but good people, and not only enjoyable or satisfying but commendable or even admirable lives are important in the ethical scheme of things.

For simplicity, let us coalesce all of the felt satisfactions of life in the area of human well-being under the rubric of welfare. It must be stressed that this is an oversimplification; people may well take satisfaction (quite legitimately) in actions or occurrences which—like Kantian works of duty—do not promote their "welfare" in any ordinary sense of that term. However, subject to this simplifying assumption, we may simply class the factors that augment the quality of life into two principal groups: the excellence-conducive and the welfare-conducive. The latter relates to objectives in the traditionally *pragmatic* range; the former are extra-pragmatic, or, as we shall call them *ideal* in nature, and relate to man's "higher" aspirations rather than to pleasure or satisfaction or happiness *per se*. Correspondingly, in assessing the quality of life, one operates with an essentially two-factor criterion in which both welfare and human excellence play a significant part.

That the quality of life cannot be assessed in terms of happiness or even welfare alone is an immediate implication of these rudimentary considerations. It is perfectly conceivable that one individual's state of personal happiness could be higher than another's (other things being equal), notwithstanding the former's lack of education, disinterest in the products of culture and the arts, and disregard of the rights and interests of his fellows. But it would not follow from this hypothesis that the individual who prospers in point of happiness or of welfare is thereby superior in "quality of life." (We come back to the cutting edge of J. S. Mill's *obiter dictum*, "Better to be Socrates dissatisfied than a pig satisfied.")

The factors that relate to excellence in quality of life need not receive much attention here. The few obvious examples adduced above—education, culture, and solicitude for one's fellows— suffice to indicate the kind of thing at issue. But one point must be stressed. The idea of "self-improvement" is both familiar and unproblematic. The aristically oriented notion that there are some things that make us *better* people stands on equal footing with the hedonically oriented notion that there are some things that make us happier people. And from the standpoint of individual or social psychology, the former concept is no more inherently intractable than the latter. What is involved in the one is just as disputable as what is involved in the other. Thus if the matter of *happiness* is to be introduced within the pale of serious inquiry, then surely the idea of *excellence* as it figures in the "quality of life" is not to be dismissed as beyond the area of possible investigation, as "unscientific" and merely a matter of subjective taste.

It is obviously appropriate and desirable that an *individual* should have life-goals that extend beyond his own welfare and that of his kindred. When one contemplates the range of the desirable achievements and accomplishments of a person, it appears that most of them do not lie within the restricted confines of welfare. Only a rather narrow band of the broad spectrum of human values falls into the region of welfare, and many values of significance fall outside. A man's aesthetic and contemplative values, for example, his being educated (along other than minimal or vocational lines), his taking on intelligent interests in the arts, or his pursuit of enjoyable avocations, are not matters that affect his *welfare* but do all the same represent important human values.[1]

For the individual person there are, or, as we have seen,

---

[1] For a basic survey of the sphere of values, see N. Rescher, *Introduction to Value Theory* (New York, 1969), especially Chap. 2.

certainly should be, important goals beyond welfare, goals whose attainment, or even pursuit, makes for a better, even if not necessarily a happier person. Examples of such goals include attainment of the respect of his associates and the love of some among them; participation in achievement in some areas of activity (vocational or avocational); appreciation of the attainments of the race in art and science; the cultivation of hobbies or sports; etc. These goals all revolve about the theme of self-development and fulfillment, a capitalizing upon the opportunities for the realization of a man's potential for appreciating and contributing to the creative impetus of the human spirit.

As the pendulum of fashion in social attitude swings, ours are hedonistic times. The tendency of the day is to worry about making people happier; it is not fashionable to talk of making them better. (We tend, at any rate, to assume this standpoint in our social outlook; at the immediately proximate environment of our own family, the perspective may be different. We want our own immediate connections—parents, spouses, children—to be *both* happy and enlightened, good people and would be reluctant to see too much of the latter be traded against gains in the former.) There is at bottom no reason why a social concern for the welfare of people should not be conjoined with a concern for the artistic dimension of life.

The pursuit of such goals lays the basis for a legitimate view of oneself as a unit of worth—a *person* in the fullest sense. And a substantial and general lack in these regards is indicative, not necessarily of any diminution of welfare, but of an impoverishment of spirit. In consequence, people as individuals have (i.e. can, should, and do have) a wide spectrum of *transwelfare goals*: the attainment of or progress toward which is definitely to be viewed as broadly speaking "in the interest" of a person, although his *welfare* might not specifically suffer from their lack. In a wholly parallel way, there are legitimate goals for a society that extend well beyond the region of the welfare of its members: in the cultivation of literary, artistic, and scientific creativity and appreciation, etc.; in the forging of an attractive and comprehensively *pleasant* life-environment; in the cultivation of congeniality in human interactions; in preserving and enhancing the appreciation of our historical, cultural, and intellectual heritage, etc.

It is important to recognize that despite its diversified and multi-faceted character, the issue of a man's welfare has a certain *minimality* about it. Welfare—in all its dimensions—deals only with the basic essentials. Insofar as the distinction between the basics and the superfluities—the necessities and the luxuries, the minimal *needs* and the nonminimal *desiderata* with respect to the constitution of a man's well-being—is operative in human affairs, welfare relates to the former items alone, without entering into the wider region indicated by the latter ones. Thus, while the components of welfare represent great, indeed essentially indispensable, assets to "the good life," they yet furnish no more than the beginnings of such a life. To possess the elemental requisites for something is not necessarily to have the thing itself. The conception of the good life represents a comprehensive whole whose range extends far beyond the core issue of welfare. The man whose cultural horizons are narrow, whose physical environment is unattractive, or whose government is despotic, may not actually suffer privation in any of the dimensions of his *welfare*—indeed, he personally may conceivably even be every bit as "happy" as otherwise. Nevertheless, we could not view his condition in point of well-being with unqualified favor and esteem his as "the good life." Welfare is only the *foundation* of such a life, not the structure itself. Physical health, adequacy of resources, and mental and emotional well-being are enormous—perhaps even indispensable—aids toward a meaningful and satisfying life, but they are not in themselves sufficient for this purpose. This is the reason why the components of the good life must extend far beyond the province of welfare.

No matter how we shape in its details our overarching vision of the good life for man, welfare will play only a partial and subsidiary role, because a satisfactory condition of affairs as to welfare is compatible with a substantial impoverishment outside the region of welfare minima. Indeed, a person, or a society, can be healthy, prosperous, and literate, but yet lack all those resources of personality, intellect, and character which, like cultivation of mind and fostering of human congeniality, make life rewarding as well as pleasant. Toward people or nations who have—even to abundance—the constituents of welfare, we may well feel envy, but our *admiration* and *respect* could never be won on this ground alone. An entire dimension of legitimate human desiderata lies beyond welfare, indeed even beyond the realm of happiness as such. For there are many things which give people *satisfaction*—perfectly legitimate satisfaction—without rendering them any *happier*. The reader of biographies cannot but become convinced that there are full and satisfying lives—eminently worthwhile lives—that are not particularly happy, but shot through with that "quiet desperation" that Thoreau perhaps mistakenly imputes to most men. And contrariwise, there are happy lives that are deplorable and may well be so deemed (quite rightly) by the persons who "enjoy" them. My aim, however, is not to dwell on these lugubrious facets of the human situation, but to stress one relatively simple and straightforward point: that any adequate vision of "the good life" for people—and for societies—must reckon with areas of human achievement wholly outside the welfare area. Neither for individuals nor for societies is "the pursuit of happiness" the sole and legitimate guide to action; its dictates must be counterbalanced by recognizing the importance of doing those things upon which in after years we can look back with justifiable pride.

The central concept of this excellence-connected, transwelfare domain is *quality*, particularly in the realization of human potentialities: in actual creativity, in the appreciation thereof, and in the forging of rewarding human interrelationships. Excellence, dignity, and the sense of worth are the leading themes throughout. Here we have left behind the domain of the minima at issue with welfare to enter another sphere—that of human ideals relating to man's higher and nobler aspirations.

3. THE LEGITIMACY OF ARISTIC GOALS

What justifies an insistence that society recognize the claims of excellence? Certainly not an appeal to social welfare: it smacks of brazen hypocrisy to argue that maintenance of art galleries, botanical gardens, theoretical physics, or the classical stage inevitably somehow advance the *welfare* of people. If the allocation of substantial social resources to museums, symphony orchestras, or institutes of advanced studies is justified—as I am convinced it is—the justification cannot proceed on the basis of welfare advancement; it should not be given with reference to

K

welfare at all (no matter how indirect), but given, rather, in terms of something else that is just as important: *an investment in social ideals.* For the very having of ideals, values, and aspirations is patently a social desideratum *in its own right.*

As the achievement of personal comfort is not enough for an individual, so the realization of the public welfare is not enough for a society. Even as a person is right to concern himself not only with his welfare, but with his *self-realization,* with "what he makes of himself" and "what sort of life he leads," so a society has—on the moral side—an inalienable obligation to foster the *quality* of its collective life. A person can realize his highest potential only when he "sets his sights" on goals that go far beyond issues relating to his standard of living. Similarly in society, the pursuit of the "higher" goals is also fundamentally important. This is something in which every member of the society has a stake—albeit a *nonwelfare* stake. For the individual this is a matter not of comfort or well-being but of self-image, self-realization, self-identity, and just plain pride. The citizen of a nation that does not neglect its duties in this area can say to himself proudly, "I am compeer to those who were in the vanguard of attaining this or that frontier of human achievement, one of those who produce the best mountaineers or sea captains of the world, one of those who first pushed the actualization of human potential toward some higher plateau in the realization of justice or the advancement of knowledge or artistic creation." What is at issue here is not a practical, utilitarian defense in terms of welfare benefits to people, but an "idealistic" defense in terms of the general principle of human ideals.

For societies, as for individuals, *transwelfare goals count*: they have a validity, legitimacy, and importance all of their own. Since the heyday of utilitarianism in the first part of the nineteenth century, the thesis that maximization of personal pleasure and its composite cousin, general welfare, is the ultimate pivot of social philosophy has gained widespread currency, even to the point of attaining the status of an established dogma. To adopt this view, however, is to overlook something very basic: the inherent incompleteness of welfare. Welfare gains its great importance as a human objective from its concern with the minimalities of a satisfactory life, but this very source of its importance marks its insufficiency as well.

4. INSTRUMENTAL VS. PRAGMATIC JUSTIFICATION: THE QUESTION OF REDUCTIONISM

The upshot of this line of thought is that the domain of our strictly practical purposes cannot validly be regarded as exhaustive of the entire range of human purposes: an extra-pragmatic dimension of legitimate human purpose must be admitted. The range of purposive justification is broader than its specifically pragmatic subdomain precisely because the range of legitimate human purpose as a whole is broader than the range of the specifically practical purposes that relate to human welfare in that it encompasses the ideal sector as well. Accordingly, *instrumental* (or *purposive*) justification in generic terms of conducing to the realization of human purpose at large is of broader scope than *pragmatic* justification in terms of specifically practical purposes.[2]

A possible argument against this position can be developed. One can maintain that practical purposes alone are ultimate, that only these have an immediate legitimacy from which all the rest are derivative. From this standpoint it would be held that all other human purposes *insofar as legitimate* can be validated as means to practical ends.

To overcome this objection we must not only recognize the *existence* of "higher," welfare-transcending purposes, but recognize them as autonomous of welfare-considerations and *legitimate in their own right*. It must thus be maintained that these purposes do not themselves require (indeed do not admit of) a pragmatic justification in terms of showing that their espousal and pursuit is conducive to practical ends. There are unquestionably good reasons for doubting that the entire range of purposes can be reduced to practical, welfare-related terms. The crucial point is that the sphere of legitimate human purpose extends beyond the narrow range of specifically welfare-oriented considerations. It

---

2 Kant certainly stressed, as sharply as one could ask for, the Humean divide between the empirical and the normative domains. But that the normative domain must itself be divided into a practical and a trans-practical area, *the former of which is ultimately the controlling force for theoretical reason* (and the latter of which is determinative with respect to ethics proper), represents a perspective that goes beyond Kantian positions in the italicized respect. Moving in the direction of pragmatic doctrines, it goes beyond pragmatism too in its recognition of an autonomous realm of value that transcends the strictly practical sphere.

is only too obvious that since the trans-welfare sector can readily *conflict* with that of welfare, there can be no reductive legitimation of the aristic sector of human purpose in terms of their being welfare-conducive.

The basis of our position is a pluralistic conception of human values that is not prepared to accept welfare and its congeners (happiness, satisfaction, "utility") as the sole pivot about which all other legitimate goals must be made to resolve, as instrumental means to this monolithic end. Instead, we see a value-pluralism that envisages a diversity and variety of intrinsic (noninstrumental) goods, insisting that one must recognize as authentic human desiderata in their own (noninstrumental) right goods which (like knowledge,[3] artistic creativity, and excellence in various lines of human endeavor) may well fail in the final analysis to prove themselves as welfare-promoting or happiness-conducive. The key point is that there exist legitimate goals whose standing is autonomous of and irreducible to the entire practical area of welfare-related considerations. Accordingly, our position espouses a fundamentally pluralistic conception of human purposes and values. It regards the purely practical sector (or welfare, happiness, satisfaction, "utility," etc.) as only one incomplete part of a larger picture, and accordingly envisages the process of means-constituting justification with reference to *these* specific ends (viz., *pragmatic* justification proper) as only one particular version of goal-oriented justification in general (viz., *instrumental* justification). The ensuing (final) chapter will be devoted to a development of this important point.[4]

---

[3] It deserves noting that there is no contradiction in holding with respect to factual knowledge that its methodological canons are validated in practical terms, but that a mastery of the substantive cognitive disciplines that result has a value which transcends the practical.

[4] This chapter has in part drawn upon the author's, *Welfare: The Social Issues in Philosophical Perspective* (Pittsburgh, 1971).

Chapter VIII

INSTRUMENTAL REASONING IN ETHICS AND THE NORMATIVE LIMITS OF PRAGMATIC JUSTIFICATION

I. THE NORMATIVE LIMITS OF PRAGMATIC JUSTIFICATION

The considerations of the preceding chapter indicate that recourse to a specifically *pragmatic* mode of instrumental justification will be apposite only in a sphere in which the precondition is satisfied that the *practical sector of purpose* (relating to the specifically welfare-oriented interests of man) is exclusively or predominantly relevant. Now the opening chapters have argued that just this is the case in the epistemology of our factual knowledge, because the purposes of the only remaining category germane to this sphere (viz., the theoretical ones) are in principle inoperative as regards justificatory reasoning here. (This contention has been crucial for the validation of the specifically pragmatic line of legitimation adopted here with respect to the epistemic methodology of our factual knowledge.) However, it now becomes clear that this presupposition of a preponderantly determinative role for practical considerations is certainly *not* appropriate in the sphere of ethics. When dealing with the assessment of human actions from the *moral* point of view, the *whole range* of human purpose must be clearly taken into account including those outside the characteristically practical sphere. Accordingly, one could not properly use a specifically pragmatic line of methodological validation approach in ethics: one could not validly argue that some method for validating ethical precepts is (*qua* method) suitable on grounds of its success in exclusively practical terms.

It is consequently worth stressing that the specifically pragmatic position taken throughout most of the preceding chapters of this book cannot properly be extended across the board. It is a valid approach only where the range of practical purposes is the controlling factor—as we have argued to be the case with respect to the epistemology of factual knowledge. But where, as certainly in ethics, the relevant range of human purposes transcends the sphere of the practical considerations that relate to our material welfare pure and simple, a specifically pragmatic analysis is not appropriate. The ultimate ground why ethics is autonomous of the realm of facts is precisely this, that the limited considerations determinative with respect to the latter are only one among other factors of which the former must take appropriate account.

2.   PURPOSIVE JUSTIFICATION IN THE NORMATIVE SPHERE

However, this argument that that specifically pragmatic justification will not prove workable in ethics (because the essential precondition of the exclusive relevance of the practical sector is *not* satisfied in this case) provides no reason to think that generically telic or instrumental justification will not work here. Let us examine in greater detail the general line of strategy to be pursued in implementing an instrumental approach. In rough outline, the course of a purposive legitimation of methods for the justification of ethical precepts would comprise the following three stages:

1. To determine (by a suitable empirical inquiry) the *actual* values and purposes that are *de facto* operative within the social group.
2. To determine (by an internal structural analysis) the *dominant* or controlling values of the group (including welfare, of course, but also its other, welfare-transcending, trans-welfare values), and then determine—through the rational scrutiny of the internal relationships among these values—the (duly rationalized) pattern of interconnections that constitutes the *value structure* of the group.[1]
3. To carry out an instrumental analysis of ethical code of the group in terms of its capacity to promote realization of the leading or controlling elements of this purposive orientation.

We must in due course consider more closely the first two items (of the determination and rationalization of the value pattern of the group). But let us first concentrate on the final and crucial item, the instrumental analysis itself.

[1] What I characterize here as the dominant values of the group comes close to what John Rawls calls the "primary social goods" in his book *A Theory of Justice* (Cambridge, Mass., 1971), pp. 90–4, and *passim* (see the Index).

As has been emphasized repeatedly in the preceding discussions, the proper sphere of instrumental justification is that of items of properly *methodological* character (tools, procedures, etc.). And accordingly, an instrumental analysis in ethics must also address itself to the legitimation of methods and instrumentalities. Its operative preoccupation is therefore not with individual actions or clusters thereof (not even when these are *purposive* in nature); rather, its concerns deal—at the essential level of methodological generality—with practices and rules or policies of acting and programs for action, all duly regarded as means to determinate ends (albeit not necessarily specifically *practical* ends). Individual actions as such are out of the picture—save, of course, at one remove—since purposive actions, duly aimed at the realization of ends, are methodological only in their generic and not their individual aspect.

Now an ethical code is to be viewed as essentially methodological on two counts: (1) in specifying the ways of *acting* in various circumstances with a view to realizing a certain conception of moral propriety, and (2) in specifying ways of *evaluating* the relative propriety of even improper actions in various circumstances, so as to provide a *standard of appraisal* for human actions. Accordingly, it is certainly possible to regard an ethical code from an instrumental perspective.

The centrally important feature of this entire line of approach is its fundamentally methodological character. Construing an ethical code as a method for the conduct of human affairs in the endeavor to realize specified objectives (which may well—nay presumably do—extend outside the practical domain), we are able to approach the issue of its legitimation through an essentially empirical determination of its effectiveness in this regard.

On first sight, of course, it is also possible to contemplate instrumental justification not just for ethical codes as a whole, but also for the individual rules or precepts that are, in effect, its constituent components. But this admittedly *possible* course of procedure is not to be favored as *appropriate*. The preferred, indeed only ultimately defensible policy is to carry out the instrumental appraisal of rules (precepts, etc.) in the wider context of the ethical code to which they belong, because this serves to determine their *conditions of application*, as well as to fix how they are to operate in situations of conflict where their implementation, though seemingly in order at first sight, is ultimately overridden by countervailing considerations. Accordingly, instrumental evaluation in the area of ethics is proper neither for specific acts nor even for isolated rules (or policies of acting), but only at the more comprehensive level of entire codes.

The methodological and generic aspect of the object of instrumentality justificatory analysis is a crucial factor on both the factual and the normative side. In the factual sphere the proper objects of instrumental validation are not particular fact-claiming *theses*, but procedures by which such theses are themselves established. On the latter, normative side, the proper object of instrumental validation is neither an act nor a rule of action, but an operational code by reference to which actions are rationalized. The level at which an instrumental justification proceeds is in both cases too general to mesh with the items of lowest (i.e., most concrete) logical status that are ultimately at issue, i.e., fact-claims on the one (factual) side, and act-directives on the other (normative) one.

3. THE CONTINGENT FOUNDATION OF HUMAN PURPOSE

Let us now return to the initial stages of the justificatory program outlined in the preceding section, the determination of the value structure of a social group.

The question of the range of human purposes cannot be settled on theoretical, *a priori* grounds. To specify the objectives that people are well advised to pursue in life demands first of all an empirical inquiry into what they say and do, and requires us to examine the facts of the matter regarding the nature of man and the character of the human condition. The pattern of human purpose roots in the contingent realities of our existence. The empirical dimension of human purposiveness must accordingly be recognized. Any serviceable clarification of the scope of people's aims and goals must root in the facts of the matter: we must begin with man as we find him and with the structure of human life as we find it. This, at any rate, must be the *starting* point—though we may ultimately hope to go beyond it by means of critical appraisal. In this area of purpose-determination we do well to adopt for the initial guidance of our first steps the bearing of Carlyle's classic *obiter dictum* regarding the lady said to have learned to accept life: "By God, she'd better." Philosophers are notoriously loath to come to grips with the empirical details of transient circumstances. It is their leading aspiration to deal with timeless truths viewed *sub specie aeternitatis*. This ideal strikes me as neither plausible nor even feasible in political and social philosophy. For the pivot point of all discussion in this region is human well-being and happiness, and this poses issues shot through with empirical detail. The point has the emphatic support of Immanuel Kant:

The concept of happiness is so indefinite that, although each person wishes to attain it, he can never definitely and self-consistently state [*in abstracto*] what he really wishes and wills. The reason for this is that all elements which belong to the concept of happiness are empirical, i.e., they must be taken from experience.[2]

In social philosophy the actualities of empirical circumstances must ever predominate.

Empirical inquiry about human values and purposes is more than a mere listing of discrete items. Above all, it requires information regarding the relative role played by these values and purposes in situations of mutual conflict. Internal relations of weight and precedence ("higher and lower") must be taken into due account. Our purposes are not created equal: some are in a dominant or controlling position *vis-à-vis* others. What is thus at issue is not just a schedule (or list) of purposes and values, but a *structure*. Within such a structure, an internal comparison of relative evaluation is definitely possible. And the realization of this possibility leads to the rational systematization of purposes and desires in the framework of an empirically based understanding of man's nature and of the human condition. (To give but one crude example, we prize *survival* more than mere *enjoyment*, and so would value—in terms of internal consistency—what is survival-conducive over what is [merely] enjoyment-conducive.)

But a crucial issue remains open. Given the (empirical) fact that a society does have a certain value, what can one say about the *genuineness* of this value. Can the "mere fact" of its being

---

[2] *Foundations of the Metaphysics of Morals* (Akad. ed., p. 418), trans. L. W. Beck (New York, 1956), p. 35.

of value show that it is deserving of recognition as normatively authentic, appropriate, and legitimate?

4. MILL'S FALLACY AND ITS LESSONS: THE "POSTULATE OF RESPECT"

Few texts in modern philosophy have received more discussion than the following passage of J. S. Mill's classic essay on *Utilitarianism*:

> The only proof capable of being given that an object is visible, is that people actually see it. The only proof that a sound is audible, is that people hear it: and so of the other sources of our experience. In like manner, I apprehend, the sole evidence it is possible to produce that anything is desirable, is that people do actually desire it. If the end which the utilitarian doctrine proposes to itself were not, in theory and in practice, acknowledged to be an end, nothing could ever convince any person that it was so. No reason can be given why the general happiness is desirable, except that each person, so far as he believes it to be attainable, desires his own happiness.[3]

A whole pack of philosophical critics have descended upon this passage of Mill's, reproving him for committing a crude fallacy in reasoning by making the move from being *desired* to being *desirable*, a step which blatantly ignores the Humean divide between fact and value, between *truth* and *norm*, between what *is* the case and what *ought* to be the case.

This matter is centrally important here. We have granted that the issue of what human purposes are is a matter of contingent empirical fact. But we are not content to let the matter rest at this factual level, seeking to obtain conclusions at the normative level of the legitimacy of purpose.

The first thing is to recognize that the step

$$\text{desired} \to \text{desirable}$$

is not a matter of an automatic inference (as, for example, in talking about whole numbers, the step from "prime" to "indivisible by 4" would be). The link is not *deductive* but *evidential*: the factual status of being desired carries evidential weight towards the normative status of being desirable. For example,

[3] J. S. Mill, *Utilitarianism* (London, 1863), chap. IV. For references to the extensive literature on the ideas of this passage see the bibliography in J. B. Schneewind (ed.), *Mill's Ethical Writings* (New York, 1965).

there is obviously a relation of a *prima facie* sort that would prevail in the absence of suitably powerful countervailing considerations. (If something is desired, then in the absence of any and all indications to the contrary, it should be recognized as desirable. In the face of the fact of desire, the burden of proof regarding desirability shifts to the other foot.) The fact of being desired is certainly not a *determinant* or guarantee of what is desirable (*worthy* of being desired, properly and warrantedly desired). But actual desire at least constitutes *presumptive evidence* of desirability, evidence that must be allowed to prevail in the absence of any counterindications, and that even otherwise must be weighted against them in the balance-scale, so as to constitute a consideration to which *some* weight must be accorded in any case. In short, though not a *guarantee* of the normative status of desirability, the empirical fact of being desired must at least be viewed as an *evidential factor* that has *some* tendency to move towards this conclusion.

But the matter does not rest there—at this simply evidential level. Considerations of respect for the worth of man and the dignity of his condition impel us towards acceptance of a practical principle along something like the following lines:

> Those purposes that people widely share in their thinking and take seriously in their actions are to be respected as legitimate.

This principle is not a factual (empirically constitutive) *thesis* about how things work in the world, but represents a procedural (normatively regulative) *postulate* as to the course of our actions: it does not say what *is the case* (viz., that these purposes *are* legitimate), it says what *is to be done* (viz., that these purposes *are to be treated as* legitimate). Its validation therefore roots in a mixture of utilitarian considerations for smoothing the channels in which human affairs run their course, and idealistic considerations—quite apart from any utilitarian implications—as to the inherent worth and dignity of man. Accordingly, it rests on what might be designated as a regulative *Postulate of Respect*—that is, respect for human dignity.[4] For the recognition by others of the propriety of one's purposes is clearly something that is in a man's interests, and respect of his personhood requires that any

---

[4] The conception of respect for persons as bearers of inherent dignity and worth is well entrenched in moral philosophy. It is a fundamental and

step which adversely affects his interests needs to be justified in terms of countervailing considerations.

The purport of this postulate is not to have us take the stance that whatever is is automatically right in the domain of human goal and purposes. The applicability of the precept is nothing automatic, but is restricted by considerations of the *appropriateness of circumstances*, with a view to such conditions as the following:

(1) the *mode* in which the purposes are held—the way in which they are subscribed to—is such as to indicate their fundamentality (e.g., through their stability).
(2) the pursuit of these purposes, while it need not advance the welfare interests of people, should not do them harm.
(3) the purposes at issue must have some deep foothold in the structure of the human condition: they should not be altogether parochial and idiosyncratic to the group in question; a wide variety of other ethical codes—even those which do not accord a comparably prominent place to the objectives at issue—must provide a background against which the according of some positive value to them can be rationalized.

We are carried back to the preceding thesis that the Postulate of Respect establishes a relationship of a *prima facie* sort that prevails only in the absence of suitably powerful countervailing considerations, considerations which the specified conditions of applicability serve to illustrate in somewhat more specific detail.

It should remove a good deal of critical sting to concede that there is nothing automatic and inevitable about the transition from "is desired" to "is desirable," but rather that this step requires due safeguards. The governing rule is that the avoidance of human frustration is in principle a morally positive good, and that in consequence the realization of our desires is also a norma-

---

pervasive theme in Kant's *Foundations of the Metaphysic of Morals* and J. S. Mill's *On Liberty*. R. S. Downie and E. Telfer, *Respect for Persons* (London, 1969) presents a stimulating contemporary treatment. See also G. Vlastos, "Human Worth, Merit, and Equality" in R. B. Brandt (ed.), *Social Justice* (Englewood Cliffs, 1962), and W. G. Maclagan, "Respect for Persons as a Moral Principle," *Philosophy*, vol. 35 (1960), pp. 193–205.

tively good thing by and large—and indeed unproblematically so in at least those cases where it does not bring normative evils in its wake. It is, accordingly, in this limited and *prima facie* sense that the Postulate of Respect is to be interpreted: to recognize something as a significant component of a complex whole is not to set it up as the be-all and end-all.[5]

The key fact about this postulate is that it affords a *bridging principle* that authorizes a move from the factual area (of "purposes people widely share and take seriously") to the normative area (of what qualifies—in subtle circumstances—as "to be respected as legitimate"). Let us be quite clear about the crucial point at issue here. We are quite deliberately flying in the face of the oft-articulated Humean dogma that there is an unbridgeable inferential gulf between matters of fact and normative matters such as those of obligation and value. We are in effect saying that under certain circumstances as to the nature of the case one can appropriately draw conclusions as to the normative propriety of certain values (purposes, etc.) on the basis of suitable factual information regarding the actualities of their espousal. But it is important to recognize that we are not passing this inferential step off as a *logical* deduction from the meaning-content of premisses, but rather as an *enthymematic* argument in which a crucial role is played by the unstated premiss afforded by a practical principle of strictly *regulative* import. The over-all force of the argument is accordingly practical in its effect rather than straightforwardly theoretical. The bridge we are erecting over the Humean gulf between fact and value affords a linkage that is a matter of practical policy rather than theoretical deduction.

It is crucial that the warranting principle at issue is *practical*, and relates to the inherently telic and norm-oriented area of human purposes. We would, of course, take a rather different view of the seemingly analogous principle:

[5] It must be stressed that we are only saying that being desired is one route to desirability, not that it is the *only* route. Something could redound to the welfare (or other proper interests) of people—and so be eminently desirable—without its ever having entered into their consciousness, let alone their actually desiring it (e.g., public sanitation in fifteenth-century Europe). Indeed, it is crucially important to our over-all argument that desire-satisfaction—which, after all, is usually of hedonic orientation—is not the only factor in establishment of desirability.

Those propositions that people widely accept in their thinking and implement in their actions are to be accepted as correct.

The critical difference between these principles resides in the classical distinction between man's will and his intellect. The point is that the very concept of a "legitimate human purpose" turns on what is *authentic for people* in terms of their actual desires and actions. On the other hand, the concept of a "correct human belief" does not turn on any aspect of man's posture *vis à vis* the world, but on "the actual facts of the matter," precisely because factual beliefs (unlike purposes, goals, aims, ideals, etc.) make another-directed claim about how things go in the world rather than an inner-directed claim about the condition of man as such. Accordingly, there is a radical disanalogy between the transition

thought to be true → actually true

and the transition

thought to be desirable → actually desirable.

Though an inferential gap certainly exists in both cases, it is far wider in the case of truth than in the case of desirability—wider not in the statistical sense that fewer people are perverse than misinformed, but in the sense of the magnitude of the added conditions to be satisfied for the transition to be properly warranted. The validation conditions for actual truth and actual desirability are such as to make for a clear and totally decisive difference between the two cases. The realm of norms and values is autonomous of "the actual facts of the matter" in a way that the realm of beliefs and truth-claims cannot be. (Though to say this is as we have seen, not to say that factual considerations do not serve as data for normative ones. They do serve as data, but their ability to do so rests on the espousal of a postulate of practical and regulative import that has no suitable counterpart on the strictly factual side.)

5.   A BRIEF RETROSPECT

The preceding discussion has made a series of points that can be put into clearer relief by viewing them in the light of three distinctions:

(i)   that between practical and ideal purposes

(ii)   that between contingent and necessary truths
(iii) that between factual and normative (evaluative) issues.

Most of our key theses can be formulated in terms of how these distinctions play off against each other:

(1) the question both of the practical and the ideal purposes that people *actually* have (cf. (i))—i.e., the consideration that there are purposes which people widely share and take seriously—falls into the domain of contingent fact (cf. (ii)).

(2) though the issue of what purposes people have is factual, a transition can be properly made from this fact to a normative (evaluative) result via the "bridging principle" that those purposes which people widely share and take seriously reserve recognition as *legitimate* purposes (cf. (iii)).

(3) that, accordingly, where human purposes are concerned the divide between the contingent and the necessary (cf. (ii)) does not run parallel to the factual/normative divide (cf. (iii)), because the concession that the entire domain of human purpose is contingent (cf. (1) above) actually provides a starting point from which we can move into the normative arena (cf. (2) above), through a recognition that *normative* necessity rests on a factual foundation.

The remaining sections will endeavor to formulate some of the implications of this strategy of invoking a practical principle of regulative import to validate a central role for factual considerations in normative inquiry. The first task is to give a brief outline of the sort of empirically based meta-ethic that results from this approach.

6.   THE STRUCTURE OF INSTRUMENTAL ANALYSIS IN ETHICS

We may begin by reiterating the earlier point that instrumental analysis in ethics leads properly to conclusions of the form not that such-and-such an act is right or wrong, but rather that such-and-such an ethical code affords a *method* for guiding the conduct of human affairs that is effective in conducing to the realization of appropriate objectives, preeminently its own, internally determinate ones. Thus, if an *instrumental* analysis is to be used in the ethical sphere (at the generic level of methodologically construed codification of practices), one must begin by determining how the appropriate range of purposes is constituted. On the account given above (§§ 3–4), this crucial issue of the structure of human purpose is to be settled by essentially empirical means, in terms of factual considerations regarding the purposes and justificatory rationale of the social group at issue. The appropriate empirical inquiry into the structure of the goals, purposes, values is not simply of the list-producing Gallup poll type, but is something much more complex and sophisticated. In subjecting materials of the Gallup poll to an in-depth analysis that reveals internal stresses and strains, it provides insight into the rational *structure* of our values and purposes. Such an analysis yields information about priority, precedence, principles of conflict resolution, etc. This serves to determine certain purposes and values as particularly basic or dominant, and accordingly specifies certain values as playing a *controlling* role *vis-à-vis* others.

At this point, instrumental analysis can be brought to bear in a more or less straightforward way. Thus, a rule of action (practice, policy of acting, etc.) that is in actual operation for a group or proposed for it can be evaluated in terms of its conducing or impeding the group's realization of its dominant purposes. (It is worth restating that this program of justificatory analysis is *instrumental* in its strategy rather than specifically *pragmatic*, because the practical area is not exhaustive of the range of legitimate human purpose.)

7.   THE LIMITS OF INSTRUMENTAL ANALYSIS IN ETHICS

One key point must be stressed: the dominant purposes themselves cannot be legitimated instrumentally: within the framework of this analysis they have to be taken as *given* and their status in effect that of *intrinsic* values. Any instrumental critique is purpose-relative: specification of the controlling purposes is an essential input, providing stable pivots around which the analysis revolves. These are thus not subject to instrumental criticism *within* the framework. Accordingly, the range of controlling purpose is itself outside the sphere of the instrumental analysis.

How serious is this limitation? It would be very serious if the range of ultimate purposes were arbitrary, which it is not. The legitimation of ultimate purposes ultimately goes back to *the very fact of their being real*—that is, their *de facto* status of being actually in force. Their very contingent reality will prove (on our approach) to be a fundamental source of their legitimacy, because the *actuality* of human purposes is—to a degree and within limits —the critical aspect of the foundations of their legitimacy.

But now it might be said even if an ultimate purpose is not arbitrary (since it is fixed by the concrete circumstances of the historical situation of a society), it is still *indifferent* because it has no inherent legitimacy, deriving its legitimacy altogether from the historical accidents of its acceptance. One seems at this ultimate level thrown back upon the old dictum "whatever is, is right." But this is *not* our position. For as the ensuing discussion of the centrality of *welfare* will go to show, this crucial factor does invariably provide a fixed basis for the Archimedean lever of evaluative criticism.

Thus while the instrumental analysis of an ethical code is in great part an inward-orientated "family-affair" of assessing it in terms of standards arrived at by an analysis of the normative situation from *its own* point of view, this is not entirely so. For it is legitimate and proper to take heed of a broad consensus among diverse codes, according them the same sort of presumptively legitimizing weight that accrues to considerations operative among the human community within which each code finds its adherents. Any ethical system which, for example, did not give a prominent place to considerations of the welfare-related area would by this very fact manifest its own inadequacy. Accordingly, a certain kind of external critique of an ethical code is possible—one external to any *given* code (though not external to the family of codes as such).

This line of legitimation places a special weight upon the welfare-related interests of man: health, adequacy of resources, benign environmental conditions, and the cognate factors that comprise the sphere of our practical concerns. Not only is it a patent fact that people in general share in prizing the cluster of values and purposes at issue here, but the way in which they function in diverse value systems lends support to the postulation that they should function among the controlling purposes of men.

Thus, the practical interests of pragmatic concern do occupy something of a special place. To be sure, they neither exhaust nor dominate the sphere of legitimate human values, but they form a substantial and central part of the complex that is stable

L

across societal lines. Our instrumental analysis does not come to destroy the pragmatic approach but to complete it; it does not reject the practical sector of human purpose and values, but only insists upon its supplementation by other values whose claims to legitimacy are no less valid.

8. THE GROUNDS OF PLURALISM IN ETHICS

There is an important difference of substance rather than structure between the instrumental analysis of methods in the factual and in the normative areas, owing to the circumstance that, unlike the normative case, there is a reasonably general consensus regarding the purposes of factual knowledge: the purely intellectual purpose of obtaining *information*, the purely practical purpose of *control*, and the mixed purpose of *prediction*. These three items provide a stable series of points of reference for the evaluative triangulation of methods in the area of fact.

These, of course, are not the only conceivable goals. But they may for all practical purposes be taken as resolved and settled within the intellectual tradition in which we define the goals of rational inquiry in the West.[6]

When, however, one turns from the factual to the normative sphere this situation becomes much less clear. For here there is nothing approaching the settled consensus as to goals and purposes that one encounters in regard to methods for the acquisition of factual information. Just what are to be the controlling purposes operative with respect to ethics? It is certainly safe enough to take the practical goals relating to human welfare to figure prominently on the list (although even here there is not an unqualified universal consensus).[7] But once we go beyond the range of welfare-related goals the situation becomes much less well-structured. All human communities agree *that* crucial purposes exist in this welfare-transcending area, but there is a substantial divergence among different groups as to just *what* these are. Unlike the rather clear-cut structure of the purposive situation in regard to human *inquiry*, that regarding human *affairs* is far less definite.

[6] Compare Sect. 9 of Chap. II above.
[7] For example as to the relative importance of the material sector of welfare *vis-à-vis* the rest.

This diversity of vision as to the controlling purposes of the interpersonal transactions governed by an ethical code is undoubtedly one basic reason why with evaluation in the sphere of action we face a situation altogether different from that encountered in the sphere of inquiry. And accordingly, the prospects that an instrumental analysis should yield results capable of commanding effectively general support are infinitely smaller in ethics than in science. But since the area of welfare-related objectives does at least constitute something of a common core, there is at least a promising prospect of applying to *some* extent the methodology of orthodoxly pragmatic justification. Let us explore this prospect somewhat more deeply.

9. INSTRUMENTALISTIC DARWINISM IN ETHICS

The line of thought we have pursued here makes it possible to discern the strand of truth in evolutionary ethics, and at the same time to see how this theory must be redesigned or reinterpreted if its claims to tenability are to be made good.

On the instrumentalistic approach, we must take a *methodological* view of ethics, so that an ethical code comes to be regarded as a body of operational precepts for the guidance of human affairs in the pursuit of specified objectives. (These objectives need not, of course, be of *practical* type, but may themselves very possibly be *ideal* in nature and have a specifically moral and aristic, rather than an even obliquely *hedonic* character relating to welfare or happiness as such.) From this standpoint, an ethic is viewed as an essentially methodological—and so purposive—instrument, as a body of injunctions and prohibitions for the practical guidance of human action towards the realization of certain goals—to wit, those that are cast in the role of its own dominant (i.e., controlling) objectives.

Given this methodological and instrumentally purpose-oriented conception of the workings of an ethical code, the question immediately arises: "But just what are the goals that are legitimately at issue here? What are the proper controlling purposes of human action?"

The entire tenor of the philosophical orientation of our discussion makes clear that the issue is not simply that of the sociological question: Just what *in empirical fact* is the goal-consensus in this or that human community? Rather the issue is that of the normative question: What can be said about those goals that are *reasonably and properly and appropriately* to be taken as operative within a community?

The key to resolving this problem lies in the factor of *survival.* Presumably in fact, and presumptively by right, a social group is fundamentally preservationist in the sense of Spinoza's *conatus se preservandi.* But it is important to recognize that what is at issue here is not simply *mere* survival: that is, the society or group seeks not only to survive, but to *survive as the sort of society it is* (relative to its own mores, practices, objectives, ideals, and values).[8] It is this *sui generis* survival as the sort of social unit it in fact is, and not survival *simpliciter*—mere physical survival— that is the determinative factor. It is a real and legitimate goal for diverse societies to pursue survival in the sense not just of the physical survival of their members, but also and no less importantly of the survival of their "way of life," which they may well rate as comparatively more significant than the physical survival of individuals.

The factor of survival *sui generis* leads to a host of further considerations that can here be indicated only sketchily, without development. For to be conducive towards this goal, a moral code must clearly be of a certain rather special sort. It must be able— under the circumstances of its operation—to reinforce those elements of social continuity and stability that make its own endurance possible. (It must thus be able, for example, to elicit a relatively ready and willing compliance, and in serving to maintain the morale and esprit of the society, it contributes crucially to its capacity for survival.) It must exhibit features of internal coherence and self-support and reinforcement that can shape and maintain a pattern of life favorable to its own continuance and towards the transmission and maintenance and promotion of those values it espouses. This requisite for the self-sustainingness of a moral code represents one of the leading factors in an

---

[8] It is worth noting that accordingly such preservationism need not automatically lead to conservationistic conservatism. If the values in view were to include innovation, change, and novelty, for example, their continued implementation may work to counter "conservatism." Depending on just what its values are, a society can thus be highly progressive, innovative, and change-seeking while continuing unmodified adherence to its "established" values and ideals.

endeavor to extend the range of the instrumental approach into the ethical sphere.

The pivotal role of survival (so construed) as a legitimate human value clearly has important implications in the context of the instrumental approach to ethics. If an ethical code is regarded methodologically as an instrumentality of goal-attainment, and if survival plays a key role in the cluster of dominant values that provides the pivot-point of instrumentalistic appraisal, then we arrive at a rationale for a version of Darwinism in ethics. Survival-conduciveness becomes a pivotal criterion of appraisal in the quest for the rational legitimation of an ethical code.[9] This position has the generic form of a social Darwinism in regard to ethics, albeit at the methodological level, rather than that of courses of action.

It is necessary to remark upon the inherent pluralism that enters at this stage. Its reference to the standard of "survival" as *sui generis* survival—rather than mere physical survival as such—makes our approach inherently pluralistic (and in a *strict* sense non-Darwinian). Because the pattern of dominant goals and controlling ideals differs from society to society, the resulting concept of instrumentalistic success in goal-realization is correspondingly variegated and lacking in uniformity. We arrive, in effect, at the pluralistic upshot that each society must be judged by its own proper standard. Cultural relativity is seemingly upon us with respect to the pattern of purpose in terms of which methods for the conduct of the affairs of a society are to be evaluated.

But it is important to realize that relativity does *not* mean arbitrariness: our position does *not* entail an indifferentist conventionalism. The fact that the controlling purposes and dominant values may vary from one society to another does not mean that they are not well-defined, determinate, and definite with respect to any *given* society. This upshot would be radically discordant with our insistence that a factualistic basis is the starting-point. After all, on our empirical line of approach, the actual,

---

[9] The caveat of our early discussion (see section 8 of chap. II) is again operative: it is not historical survival as such that is itself crucial, but only survival as an indicator of survivability. Thus, survival itself is only the starting-point for this neo-Darwinian approach: the circumstances of this *survival* must be such that it can reasonably be construed as providing the rational warrant for a postulation of *survivability*.

current historical situation provides the specification of the relevant range of purpose. Its point of view is the thesis that in determining the range of purposes, ideals, and values of the society, one cannot but "go on from where we are"; that in this regard those standards that are actually "in possession," as it were, have in large measure the backing of situational legitimacy. The structure of norms operative in a society is not a thing of haphazard, but is fixed for it in a definite form by an historico-evolutionary process. The crucial feature of the pattern of values and purposes of a society is an historically conditioned definiteness, not an indifferentist arbitrariness. Languages do differ from one culture to another, but that does *not* mean that it's a matter of indifference which language one speaks *within* a culture. To be in and of a culture is to enter into its norms. On this approach one sees in clear perspective the aspect of truth in Hegel's thesis that history is the arbiter of human standards, in that the concrete history of any culture serves in substantial measure to define the standards of purposive evaluation that must be accepted as appropriate to it. The social order that is given provides a basis of specificity that *prempts* any intrinsic indeterminacy of absolutes.

But not only does our cultural relativity regarding purpose-frameworks avoid conventionalistic indifferentism, but it is well worth stressing that the scope of this relativism is itself of a limited sort. In maintaining that survival *sui generis* is indeed a controlling purpose of effectively universal scope (as we have done), physical survival comes to be cast willy-nilly in a highly important role. For physical survival is patently requisite for any other sort of survival: no mode of preservation can be achieved without it. Accordingly, physical survival must play an important role in any rational structure of social purpose. Human welfare, with its stress on the material conditions of man's existence (health, resources, security), is accordingly a pivotal factor of essentially universal scope.

The prominent (though not predominant) role that material welfare is bound to have within the range of the controlling purposes of societies—a role that gives it in effect something of a universalist standing which transcends the more parochial limits of other considerations—points to the elements of truth that our position is prepared to discern in evolutionary ethics. The grain of truth in evolutionary ethics is simply this, that while the welfare-oriented survival-conductiveness of an ethical code is by no means the sole, or even necessarily the all-predominating, factor among the operative validating credentials, it is invariably one of the small handful of maximally relevant items which *any* rational analysis of legitimating factors must be prepared to take into account in a detailed and serious way.

Such a recognition of the centrality of welfare and material well-being as a human objective of virtually universal scope must not be distorted: its importance as *one* of the controlling factors (to be sure one of uniquely general scope) should not be exaggerated into setting it up as the be-all and end-all. It is an important part of a wider complex, rather than a toti-subordinating pivot-point around which all other considerations must revolve. It is exactly around this point—the need to supplement specifically practical (welfare-oriented) considerations by others relating to different but equally valid human objectives—that the important difference between the generically instrumental and the specifically pragmatic evaluation of methodological instrumentalities revolves. But the fact that the basic considerations of welfare need to be *supplemented* in a wider framework of legitimate human values does not mean that they can be *ignored*.

10. CONCLUSION

The straightforwardly instrumental line we have taken with respect to ethical codes puts the justificatory situation here into a close parallelism with our pragmatic validation of the foundations of factual knowledge. But "parallel" does not mean "contiguous," and in fact a vast gulf still remains between the two. This is so because, whereas the range of ethically relevant purposes is highly polychromatic, the practical range of purpose is alone determinative in the latter, factual case. In taking the methodological view of the rational foundations of fact-oriented epistemology, we give a decisive predominance to the role of man's factual beliefs as navigation-aids through the shoals and narrows of the natural world. This function of practical considerations as the decisive controlling factor on the factual side does not carry over to the normative side, and can be taken to do so only on pain of gross injustice to the wider range of human concerns to which any viable ethic must give due recognition.

Precisely because specifically *pragmatic* reasoning proceeds on a far narrower basis than telic or instrumental reasoning of the generically purposive sort, the present instrumentalist approach in ethics—which countenances the controlling role of purposes outside the pragmatic/hedonic range—is of broader scope than the traditional hedonistic pragmatism. This instrumentalistic strategy of justificatory analysis is, however, akin to pragmatism and to evolutionary ethics in its factual approach to values. Despite this, it is not, however, puristically anormative and "value-free," because it is in a position to *criticize* the factually determined purposes and values from two perspectives. One line of criticism is strictly internal to the value-scheme, proceeding by a dialectic of consistency with reference to certain controlling values (as determined empirically in terms of the relative weight which that value-scheme itself assigns to various values, norms, and purposes in situations of conflict). The other line of criticism is (at least in principle) external and proceeds with reference to those evaluative concepts which function prominently across a wide range of diverse value systems—in particular and most decisively the pivotal concept of human welfare. The resulting method of instrumentally justificatory analysis in ethics is inherently pluralistic and culture-relative, but tempers its relativism and pluralism by a stress on interculturally uniformitarian considerations on the side of human welfare. This approach thus handles normative considerations largely in terms of issues that fall on the straightforwardly factual side of the traditional division between normative values and empirical facts.

NAME INDEX

SUBJECT INDEX